The Rain May Pass

The Rain May Pass

ALAN SHAYNE

RAND-SMITH PUBLISHING
ASHLAND, VA USA

THE RAIN MAY PASS

Print ISBN: 978-1-950544-18-9
Digital ISBN: 978-1-950544-19-6

Registered with the Library of Congress

Cover design courtesy of Norman Sunshine

Rand-Smith Publishing
www.Rand-Smith.com
Ashland, VA

Printed in the USA

Contents

For Norman

Acknowledgements

First I want to thank Random House's great Kate Medina for making me realize that "A book has to be its own reward. Just the creation of it, the pursuit of one's own creativity, is what really matters, and it is what illuminates and adds meaning to life. To recapture and make some kind of sense of the past is so valuable and is what so much of Literature shows us."

I thank my friends Glenn Jordan and Michael Kahn for pointing out the things that were missing and the ones that needed to be removed.

Ene Riisna Greenfield read version after version and always coaxed me on as did Susan Nernberg and Lee Wolf.

To Diane Nine for being a ten as my agent.

A special thanks to David Smitherman to contributing so much in his edit and finally, his belief in the book.

Norman Sunshine is not only the end of my thanks but the beginning and middle as well.

Chapter 1

I'd spent every summer of my life on Cape Cod since I was a baby. My mother said she used to swim the length of Falmouth Heights every day when she was pregnant with me. In a way, I felt it was more my home than Brookline where we lived in the winter. Lots of rich people from Boston had summer homes on the Cape.

We didn't have much money, so my parents rented a run-down caretaker's house behind my uncle and aunt's property. It wasn't much, but at least we got away from the heat and my dad could drive just a couple of hours when he had to be in the city. There wasn't air conditioning in those days, and our apartment was on a street with truck traffic and overlooked three gas stations, so the Cape was like being in paradise.

During my fifteenth summer, everything changed. My brother was in college. I wasn't a kid anymore, and the house we rented in Falmouth had been torn down, since my aunt and uncle had died. So, my parents weren't going to go there anymore. They wanted me to go, but I'd have to stay with my grandmother and work in her gift shop. I didn't mind working but being with her for two months would be a nightmare. She was anything but the lovable "granny" I used to see in the movies. Besides, she didn't seem to like me or anyone else for that matter.

After we finished supper one night, I said to my parents for probably the tenth time, "I don't want to go to Falmouth."

"You're going," my father said. He didn't even look up from the kitchen table. He was too busy with his health magazines.

"But why?" I replied. "Why can't I just spend the summer here? I can go to the beach with a couple of my friends and I can do some studying. I won't be any trouble." I'm sure he knew this was just a ploy, but it was worth a try.

"We want you to get away from all this heat. You can swim there, and it will be much healthier for you." My father always acted as if I was some kind of invalid, but he was obsessed with the whole family's health. "I told you before, someone has to be with your grandmother. She's getting older and she needs help in the shop. Besides, she's going to pay for your room and board. It'll be a free vacation."

My mother was washing dishes at the sink. She said nothing. I knew she wasn't in favor of my going at all. She didn't get along with my grandmother and she must have known how dreary it was going to be. I reached out to her as a final resort. "Mother, I can help you around the house and I can get a part-time job. They always need kids to scoop ice cream at St. Clair's in the hot weather."

"I have nothing to do with this," she said. "Your father has made up his mind and there's no changing it. If you're miserable, I'll see what we can do, but you have to at least give it a try."

I gave up. I'd have to spend the whole summer with a person who was unpleasant and cold. Well, what could I do? I tried to look on the bright side. Maybe something good would come of it.

At that time, I was really a kid. I even kept a diary that I wrote in every day. I used to share my bedroom with my brother, but now he had a place in Boston where he was going to Northeastern University. He only came home now and then to learn photography with my father, so I had the room all to myself. My parents could burst in anytime they wanted to though, so I had to hide under the covers with a flashlight in my left hand as I wrote. That night, I opened the little red book with 1941 stamped on the cover and turned to the blank page for June 21. I thought for a minute and then began to write:

Well, today was a lucky day. School is all over –

Year's marks: Math – A, Span – B, Lit – A, Comp – B, Mech. Dr. – A

They're mailing my report card. I had to pay seventy-five cents for my lock in the gym that Mr. Bemis said I didn't return, but I did. He

always picked on me whenever he could. At least I don't have to see him
for a few months.

Vi un paseo con Irving L. Compramos ice cream cones. Vimos unas
muchachas hermosas y les hablamos. In eve, Irving and I went over
Sandra Powers house and visited she and Barbara Berger. At first, I
didn't recognize Barbara – in fact I was so stunned by her improved
appearance I was in a daze for a period after I met her. Finland
may declare war on Russia. Tomorrow, Mom and Dad are driving me
to Falmouth where I will help my grandmother in her shop for the
summer.

I started to put the cap on the fountain pen and changed my mind. Instead, I very carefully drew a symbol in the margin. It was the letter T sitting on top of a small circle because I was trying not to play with myself too much. I thought by putting the symbol in my diary every time I did it, it would remind me to control myself more. So far, it wasn't doing much good. I turned off the flashlight and reached for my penis.

The next morning, I could hear my parents' voices through the door as I was packing my suitcase in my bedroom.

"Dearie," my mother said, "I can't find Mother Schein's medicine. Have you got it?"

"No," Dad replied, "I left it on the sink in the kitchen."

"Will you get it for me?" she asked.

"I can't," he said, "my hands are dirty. I'm shining my shoes."

I heard my mother's sigh of exasperation. My father was a clean freak, and he always worried about getting germs. "It's just a bottle. You can't hurt it," she said.

"All right," my father sounded annoyed, "just wait until I wash my hands."

There was a sound of my mother slamming down whatever she was holding. "Never mind," she said, "I'll get it myself."

I listened to see if either of them was about to come into my room. The silence told me they were probably sulking as they usually did after one of their minor battles. I went over to the wall where I had hung a picture of a clipper ship. When my brother left, I had asked for wallpaper patterned with ships so that I'd feel like I was on a boat. I'd found this print and a cheap frame to put it in. I took it down and placed it on the bed. I peeled back the metal hinges that held the backing in place and removed the cardboard. This was where I hid things so no one would find them.

I took out a stack of photographs. The top ones were nudes of a girl standing in front of a maple tree. Each picture was a different pose. She wasn't very pretty, but she sure looked sexy. I looked at each picture quickly and then put them on the bed. At the bottom was a closeup of a naked boy being held by two older boys wearing clothes. They were laughing as they forced the younger one to show his penis to the camera. I'd added that picture recently. It seemed kind of sexy to me, like the *Strength* and *Health* magazines I'd steal a glance at in the bookstore when the owner wasn't watching. I looked at the picture and then put the frame back together and hung it on the wall. I scooped up all the other pictures and hid them in my suitcase below my underwear. I closed the latch and set the suitcase by the door.

I was ready to go.

Chapter 2

It took almost an hour before the car was packed that day. It was a 1937 Willys, and it was very small. My bicycle had to be tied on the back bumper with blankets wrapped around it so it wouldn't scratch Dad's precious car. Then there were the suitcases, bags of food, and kerosene stove for my father's vegetarian meals. He wouldn't eat sandwiches, so my mother had to cook him special things. He ate a meat substitute made from soybeans. He made me taste it once saying it was just like hamburger. It sure wasn't. I could barely get it down, and I refused to eat it ever again.

We kept putting things in the backseat and shifting them around until we could find the right combination so there'd still be enough room for me. By then it was getting late, and my mother's face was pinched and angry. "I was ready at eight-thirty," she said as we drove away from the apartment.

"Well, I was ready," replied my father.

"Why didn't you say something?" she snapped.

"What do you mean, why didn't I say something?"

"You were reading your health magazines. The least you could have done is pack the car—"

My father stopped her. "Let's not discuss it. Let's try to enjoy the day."

I sat quietly in the back. The last thing I would ever do is take sides, but I noticed my father didn't say, "Let's enjoy the day." He said, "Let's try to enjoy the day," because they never did.

The trip took three hours though Falmouth was only eighty miles from Brookline. My father was a very careful driver and lunch took an hour by the time we unpacked the stove and Mother had cooked Dad's disgusting soy burgers. They had another fight when my father found some classical music on the radio that he usually played only on Sundays.

"Must you play that dreary music?" Mother asked him. "It gives me a headache."

Dad replied, "Can't you ever try to improve your mind?" They stopped talking after that entirely.

At that time, I couldn't understand why they just didn't seem to get along. They slept in the same bed. Once, I found a book of postcards they had sent each other when they were engaged, and Mother was living in Kansas and Dad was in Boston. They were so lovey-dovey. I also discovered a book about woman's health hidden away in the back of the bookcase. Inside was a list of dates Mother must have written. I guess it had something to do with when they had sex because it was hidden in a chapter on that kind of stuff. But there was this tension between them, almost like heat lightning in the summer that makes you keep waiting for the storm.

When we started driving again, things kept falling down in the back seat. I had to hold them in my lap because I had no luck in shoving them back in place. By the time we were close to the Cape, I was buried in boxes and bags.

It was a gray day but that didn't dampen my excitement. I kept looking out the window, waiting for the special landmarks that told me how much farther we had to go: the stone pillars on either side of the road, the Dutchland Farms where we'd sometimes stop for small boxes of ice cream with wooden spoons tucked inside, the "Herring Run" sign, and the open-air dance hall in Buzzards Bay.

When I finally saw the stone pillars, my heart leapt. We were in Wareham. Any minute we'd be in Buzzards Bay, and I suddenly thought I didn't care if my grandmother was awful. She couldn't take away from what I felt about being back. As we drove into Buzzards Bay, I saw the dance hall. Every year when we passed it on our way, I thought *someday I'm going to go dancing there when I get old enough.* The paint was peeling badly on the "Blue Moon" sign and it looked deserted, but I figured it would look good when they fixed it up.

The season didn't really begin until the Fourth of July weekend, and everything was always done at the last minute.

We crossed the Bourne bridge over the Cape Cod Canal. The railroad bridge in the distance was high in the air. A ship must have just gone through. At last, we were on the Cape. Straight ahead was nothing but scrub pine woods on either side of the road. I was excited, as if something wonderful was going to happen. I always felt that way when we finally reached the Cape. Maybe it was the smell of the sea, but it was a whole different feeling than I felt anywhere else. It was a sense of freedom.

"I have the worst heartburn," my mother said.

"That's because you get aggravated," my father replied. "Why do you upset yourself?"

"You know," she answered, "your mother has been waiting all day. She'll be frantic."

"We'll get there. Don't worry." Then he went on. "I wish you'd stop drinking coffee in the morning."

"Dearie, please," she said as if she knew what he was going to say next, "that doesn't give me the heartburn."

"Why don't you just try my coffee substitute for a few days? I know you'll feel a hundred percent better."

"I can't stand the taste of it."

"It tastes exactly like coffee," he sounded shocked. "Everybody says it does. You just won't give it a chance."

"Please, I've got to have my coffee. I have few enough pleasures as it is."

My father was not to be stopped. "At least you could use the soy milk instead of cream."

I stopped listening and just stared out the window.

At last, I saw the sign that said "Falmouth." I watched the shabby houses go by and change into bigger and better ones as we got closer to town. We went past an old country store that had been brought from upstate New York and put on the plot of land where we used to live when I was growing up. I knew the guy who owned it. When he was finished, he was going to sell antiques there. It looked pretty awful now, but I guessed there was still a lot to do. He had already torn down the house we rented that wasn't any good anyway.

The big house next door where my Uncle Louis and Aunt Rae lived was still there, though they had died. My Aunt Rae had something wrong with her that made her say all her thoughts out loud. If we went to dinner there, she'd serve you food and say, "Have some more potatoes." Right after that she'd say out loud, "Why should I wait on these people? They keep eating all our food and they don't do a damn thing." She didn't know she was saying it, so nobody paid any attention, but it was weird. I had to keep from laughing, but I felt sorry for her too.

Finally, we rounded a corner that curved away from the highway and came to a group of buildings where my grandmother had her shop. A sign read, "Queens Byway," and on one side of the road were four shops. My grandmother's was the one next to the parking lot. Beside hers was Goodell's Dress Shop, and next to that was a candy store. The fourth shop was empty. Across the street, there were other shops, but they were more elegant, and one was a fancy dress shop that some wealthy people owned.

Nana's shop had two huge windows with small panes to make it look like it was from the eighteenth century. The bright red wooden door was ajar, but there was a sign taped to it that read, "Opening July 1." Inside, I could make out a mess of tables heaped with merchandise, boxes, and wrappings. I could see my work was cut out for me. The other shops still had paper pasted on the inside of the windows left over from the winter. Those owners hadn't returned yet.

Dad parked the car in front of the store, and we piled out. He opened the screen door and yelled, "Mother, Mother!"

My grandmother appeared through a curtain tacked over a doorway in the back of the shop. She was chewing, and in her hand was a piece of rye bread covered with her favorite—cottage cheese. She had on an oversized sweater that she hadn't bothered to button. Her blouse was spattered with food stains. Her dark skirt was smudged with the same powder that caked her sallow cheeks. Once, at the train station in Florida where my Uncle Sumner sent my grandmother every winter, a woman nearby whispered, "Look, there's a Seminole Indian." With her multi-colored clothes and shopping bags full of old stockings that she made into rugs, my grandmother was certainly unusual looking.

My father made a kissing sound next to her face, but his mouth was as far from her as possible. My mother didn't go near her, but she did say "Hello, Mother Schein." I thought I really had to, so I kissed her cheek as I said, "Hi Nana."

"You said you'd be here early," she glowered at my father.

"We got a late start," Dad replied. "It's all right. We have all day tomorrow to help you." She gave him a dirty look. "Now," he tried to get it all back to normal, "where do you want everything? I have the medicine in a separate bag."

"The clothes have to go to the house," Grandma said. Her accent and her false teeth made her pronounce every word carefully. "It's too late to go. We don't have time to get there before supper. Mrs. Hotchkiss stops serving at seven."

"We might as well eat now, then," my mother said.

"If I'd known we were going to eat so early, I wouldn't have had my tea," my grandmother muttered.

"We have a little time left," Dad said. "Let's at least take whatever you want into the shop."

We started unloading the car. It wasn't easy since the tables and showcases took up almost every inch of the shop. The narrow path around them was almost like a maze. At a certain point, you had to turn back and retrace your steps to go in another direction.

The tables were covered with various objects: Mexican dishes, baskets, Chinese cloisonné and Italian Della Robbia plaques (I learned the names for both when I worked part-time in the shop the summer before), cheap jewelry, knitted bags, dolls, ash trays, and cigarette boxes. The only things that had any connection to Cape Cod were a sea captain doorstop, a Cape Cod barometer and some cranberry pickers that held magazines. Everything was a mess, with excelsior on the floor and boxes half unpacked. We could barely squeeze by the tables to carry everything to the back room. It was also jammed with merchandise, along with a cot for Nana's nap and a two-burner stove. We stacked all the stuff in a huge pile and decided to sort it in the morning.

We'd taken so many things into the store that there was now room in the car for all of us. I helped Nana get into the back seat and we set off for dinner. It turned out to be a place right around the corner and we could have walked in the same time it took us all to get into the car. It was a room-and-board in a huge white house that looked at least fifty years old. Outside, there was a weather-beaten sign swinging in the wind that read "Elm Tree Inn." We parked and walked up the steps to a screened porch with about ten tables and green wooden chairs. It was still too cold to eat outdoors though, so we went into what once must have been the living room and was now the main dining room.

A fat woman with an Irish brogue right out of a vaudeville sketch came rushing to greet us. "You're very late," she said sternly, and then she broke into a toothless smile. "So, you're the family," she wiped her right hand on her apron, "I'm Mrs. Hotchkiss." Then she shook hands with each one of us. I could see that Dad didn't want to shake hands with her and get her germs, but he was trapped. I watched him try to get away from her, but he finally had to put out his hand. My mother, in her usual way, tried to be friendly, "Mother Schein has told us how nice you've been to her."

"I don't believe it," Mrs. Hotchkiss interrupted. "She doesn't have a kind word for anyone, but we put up with her." She laughed raucously. "Now sit down, sit down while we have something left in the kitchen." She passed around some hand-written menus.

"I don't see anything but meat and chicken," my father said.

"Ralph," Mother said, "a little piece of chicken won't hurt you."

"I'll just have some vegetables and a little soup," he said to Mrs. Hotchkiss.

"And a small piece of chicken," Mother added.

"I don't want it," Dad insisted, "don't make an issue."

"Do you not eat meat then?" Mrs. Hotchkiss sounded amazed.

"Not if I can help it."

Mrs. Hotchkiss made a face. My grandmother interrupted, "Is the lamb well done enough for me?"

"You better have that," Mrs. Hotchkiss said. "I know you won't like it, but it's the best thing for you tonight." She turned to my mother. "Oh, how we have to put up with her." She laughed her crazy laugh again, "You got a nice boy here." She patted me on the shoulder. "I got a boy too," she said, pointing at a balding man who was waiting on a table nearby. "That's Eddie." He heard his name and turned to face her. "What are you looking at?" she said to him. "Get on with your work and get those people to order. I'm not keeping my kitchen open all night. Now get going and take your little farts with you." Eddie turned abruptly and left the room, and Mrs. Hotchkiss screamed with laughter.

We ate in silence. My grandmother hunched over, slurping her food and making noises with her false teeth. My mother had long ago given up being anything but civil to her. When I was a child, we lived in my grandmother and grandfather's house. My parents would fight because my mother had to do all the cleaning and cooking, and my grandmother never lifted a finger. All she did was complain that the food wasn't any good or the house wasn't clean enough. I fell asleep every night hearing my mother beg my father to get her away from that house.

Finally, when I was eleven, my grandfather died, and we got an apartment in Brookline. There wasn't room for my grandmother, and she began to spend her winters in Florida and her summers in Falmouth. My mother never forgave her, and my father didn't seem to feel anything toward her. Now he barely spoke to her. He just picked at the food on his plate and chewed it daintily.

I looked around at the other guests. They were all fifty or sixty years old. These were the people I would spend the next two months with. I stared out the window at lilac bushes that were now dripping with rain.

The rooming house where Nana lived was on the main road about a mile north of the Elm Tree Inn. We must have passed it on our way into town. It was a shabby, narrow frame house in the poorer section. There was a sign stuck into a patch of neglected grass in front of it that read "Guests" with a naked lightbulb on either side of it. The lights weren't on inside, so Dad aimed the car at the house so we could unload my suitcase and the clothes Grandma had asked for. The landlady, a painfully thin woman in her sixties, finally appeared and held the door open for us, but even so, Dad and I were soaked from the rain by the time we got everything in.

My parents were going to sleep in my room for the night, and I would sleep in an alcove off of my grandmother's room. I took my suitcase upstairs and the landlady followed me and turned on a light. Inside was a tiny dressing room with a single cot and no window. When everybody got settled, I undressed and got into bed. My grandmother was only a few feet away from me. I looked straight at a glass of water with her teeth in it on her bedside table. If that weren't enough, as I started to fall asleep, Nana began a series of snores, wheezes, and choking sounds. At least, when my parents left, I'd have a room of my own.

Chapter 3

When I woke up, the sun was out, and we all went to work cleaning the shop. I washed the tiny panes of the windows and Dad unwrapped Mexican dishes that he gingerly removed from a large basket, holding each one away from his body. I knew he was trying desperately not to get any foreign germs on himself. My mother swept the worn carpet that covered most of the floor. We were all busy and no one said a word until my grandmother attacked my mother. "Do you have to make so much dust?" she said. "It's getting all over the jewelry I'm trying to put away."

She had been baiting my mother all morning and mother had had it. "How else can I get rid of this filth?" she answered.

My grandmother wasn't going to let it go at that. "Couldn't you sweep a little easier? It's getting over everything."

Mother snapped back, "Are you telling me how to sweep? If you know so much about sweeping, how come you never sweep this rug?"

Nana tried to grab the broom from my mother. "Here, give it to me," she said. "I'll do it!"

Mother kept the broom. "Leave me alone."

My grandmother managed to grab the handle. "You don't have to help me," she said, "I don't need your help. I'll do it myself."

They began a tug of war until suddenly Mother jerked the broom away from Nana and threw it on the floor. It made a sound like a shotgun blast. "Oh, for God's sake, take it," Mother said as she stomped out the side door into the parking lot.

Nana turned to my father, "What's the matter with her? She doesn't have to do me any favors. I don't need help from any of you."

"Mother," pleaded my father, "don't aggravate yourself."

I just went on washing the windows. I'd seen so many of these fights. At least they always went back into their corners afterward. Maybe now it would be quiet for the rest of the time.

I thought the day would never end, but it finally did. The shop didn't look that much better, but I guess it was a little cleaner. Nana had so much junk that every inch of every table was covered with something. By the time I dusted one table and moved to the next, the first one was dusty again. We only stopped working when it was time for dinner at Mrs. Hotchkiss'.

After another meal with nobody talking to each other, my parents were ready to drive back to Brookline. First, they took Nana to the rooming house while I rode my bike that we'd finally unloaded from the back of the car.

When I got to the house, Mother and Dad were waiting to say goodbye and give me instructions for the summer. "Be sure to be careful with your bike," my father said. "I let you ride it tonight, but from now on when it gets dark, walk it back here, don't ride it." I could see myself dragging my bike back to the rooming house that was at least a mile from the shop and the Elm Tree Inn. Besides it had a perfectly good light, but I didn't say anything. My father wasn't done. "Don't go swimming where the water is over your head. There could be one of those currents that take you out to sea. Don't be a smart aleck and show off just because the other kids have to swim out where it's deep."

My mother smothered me with kisses I hated but had to put up with. "Oh, I love you so much, oh I love you so much," she kept repeating. I heard her once say the same thing in the same way to our dog. "I'm going to miss you so," she went on.

My father interrupted her. He wasn't done with me yet. "Don't do too much exercise and don't eat too much meat!" There was the invalid theme again.

We were standing in front of the rooming house and Nana, who was being ignored, got annoyed. "For heaven's sake, go if you're going. It's getting cold."

I'd already had enough hugs and kisses from my mother so I just

I kissed my father perfunctorily on the cheek. They got into the car and I waved as they drove off. Then I followed my grandmother into the house.

I locked the door as soon as I got into my room. I'd never had a room with a lock before and it made me feel like I was grown up at last. Now nobody could walk in on me and I could do whatever I wanted. I took everything out of my suitcase and put it in neat piles in the chest of drawers. For the time being, the nude pictures found a home in the drawer of a small table next to the bed. I would need to find another place to hide them when the woman came to clean.

My room had four windows—one directly on the highway, two facing the highway so as cars approached their lights shone directly in, and one facing the backyard. All of the furniture was pretty drab and worn. There were white beaverboard walls, glass curtains, green paper shades in the windows, and cheap, dingy white spreads on the twin beds. Homemade braided rugs were scattered on the floors.

After unpacking, I got into my pajamas and took my diary and a pen to bed. I propped two pillows against the headboard, leaned against them and opened the book to June twenty-third. I drew my capital letter T and the circle underneath. Then I reached for the nude photographs from the bedside table.

Chapter 4

The next day, I started a ritual that only changed on Sundays. After I got up, I took a shower and dressed, bicycled a mile to the store, had some juice and coffee, and then began to work. I wanted to make the store look as good as the other stores on the Byway. It was a hopeless task, but I felt I had to do it.

My grandmother always ordered too many things from the salesmen who flattered her. As a result, there wasn't enough room on top of the tables in the shop to put all the merchandise that arrived, so she shoved a lot of it underneath them. Cloths with India prints covered the tables and went all the way to the floor so nobody could see the mess. The trouble was that when Nana wanted something from under one of the tables, she pulled out all the boxes, like an animal digging for food, and everything was thrown around until she found what she was looking for. Then she'd grab onto the table, hoist herself up, and walk away.

I'd have to clean it all up and put everything back. When that was done, I'd sweep the broad sidewalk in front of the store and arrange the Mexican baskets and brightly colored red and blue chairs under the multi-paned windows. Then came my favorite moment when I'd stop and admire my handiwork and take a few deep breaths of the delicious fresh air before returning indoors to face the dust and disorder again.

Each day, I chose one long table to work on. First, I dusted everything and tried to arrange the articles as attractively as possible. My grandmother just piled everything on top, as she unpacked the boxes when they arrived, so there was no order or form to please the eye. I tried to find some beauty among the pottery candlesticks, cherubs holding bud vases, black carved Mexican boxes, Orrefors glass, demitasse cups, doorstops and many other items. I weeded out a lot of cheap things from the good merchandise and set it on a nearby table. Then that table had to be straightened out, so I would move things from one place to another.

Instead of thanking me for all I did, my grandmother put everything back the way it was in the first place, restoring the jumble she seemed most comfortable with. "Nana," I said, "please don't make a mess again. I just straightened that table."

"It's better the way it was," she replied.

"But nobody can see anything the way it was," I said.

"I can see it," she said.

Oh God, I thought, she's impossible and I have to stand this for the whole summer. In time, I realized she was probably right. The mess was good for business. Once we opened the shop, most of the people who came in had heard the store was a place for bargains. They sifted through the odd mixture on the tables looking for treasures as if they were at a flea market. Nothing had a price tag, so the word spread you could haggle with the old lady on the Byway. They treated her as if she were an Arab in the bazaar. They weren't far from wrong.

Nana wouldn't let anyone get out of the shop until she'd made a sale. She often sold things under cost because she never wrote anything down and didn't remember what she had paid. She always showed a loss at the end of the summer, but my rich Uncle Sumner, who paid for everything, was glad to keep her in the shop and as far away from him as possible.

After a week of fighting Nana about fixing the inside of the shop, I gave up. I was restless. I didn't know any kids my age or any grownups for that matter, except my grandmother and she barely spoke to me. During the day, if no customers were there, she sat in the back of the store reading cheap love stories she got at the lending library. If she wasn't reading, she was making tea on the two-burner stove or smearing rye bread with cottage cheese. At night, I would sit opposite her at Mrs. Hotchkiss' and watch her somehow get the food past her false teeth. They kept sliding down from her gums, but when they did work, they made a clicking sound that I was sure everyone at the other tables could hear.

Once in a while, I'd leave to get some air and look in the other shop windows. One by one, they began to open as the season was getting started. I noticed that along the parking lot, next to Nana's shop, was a small section of dirt that was shielded from the cars by some bushes. The screen door from the store opened onto it. I thought it would be a perfect place for a small garden. I told Nana about it, but of course, she wasn't interested.

I said, "Nana, it's a great place for you to sit and read your books. I'll put your chair out there. You'll get a little air and you can hear the customers coming in. Just give me a dollar and a half, and I'll plant some flowers. You'll have your own garden."

"It's too much money. It's ridiculous," she said.

I kept pestering her until she finally gave in. "All right," she said, "I'll give you the money, but I won't sit out there."

I planted a row of petunias and placed Nana's wooden chair opposite them. It looked really nice. She refused to go to my little garden at first, but finally, because she had nowhere else to sit, she grudgingly took her romance books outside. I tended to the flowers often and they thrived for a short time. Nana sat there every day for a while, but I noticed that she never looked at the flowers. It didn't take long for the fumes of the cars in the parking lot to kill the petunias and for me to bring Nana's chair back inside. There was no point in asking her for more money. She didn't let me forget how much I had already spent and that she'd gotten nothing out of it.

I waited on customers most of the day. They were usually older women with blue hair who said I was "cute." I had to ask Nana the price of anything a customer was interested in. Rather than tell me, she moved in quickly to take over the sale. Her eyes would narrow craftily, and she would purse her mouth to control her eagerness. However, she wasn't a match for the women who kept cutting her down to get one of her famous bargains. The whole thing embarrassed me and since she made most of the sales, I didn't feel I was accomplishing anything.

Chapter 5

At last there was some activity in the store next door. I looked out the window and saw a van draw up in front of it. A kind of good-looking Irishman, around forty, got out and started to lug dresses into the shop. It wasn't that hot, but this guy was sweating like a pig. His face was red and blotchy. Then Mrs. Goodell, who I'd known slightly for many summers, opened the door by the driver's seat. She didn't look so well. She was kind of horse-faced and big-boned, and now she seemed a lot older. She obviously wasn't happy with the way the man was working. She grabbed an evening dress as it started to trail on the sidewalk and swooped down on a belt that fell out of a garment bag. I heard her loudly giving him instructions that he seemed to ignore.

I went outside thinking I'd say hello and offer to help. But they had disappeared, so I went back into the store. The next day, I ran into Mrs. Goodell who greeted me with, "How handsome you've gotten, Alan." I was surprised she even remembered my name. "How's your mother?" she asked.

"Fine," I said.

"We have to have a good visit, but I'm so busy now getting the store ready. As soon as we're squared away, I want to know everything you're up to." She grabbed my chin and pinched it. "See you soon." She rushed off and for the next few days, the doors to her shop were always closed and I didn't run into her. The paper in the windows disappeared eventually and when I walked by, there were female mannequins all dressed up and the place looked pretty elegant.

A few days later, as I was setting out the baskets in front of the store, a 1930's roadster with the top down came zooming around the corner from the highway. It tore past the blinker, set in an island to separate the traffic lanes, sped into the parking lot, and hit the brakes suddenly, just a few feet away from me. A young girl in her twenties with a very short haircut that looked like she'd cut it herself, was driving. She had a pert, upturned nose and seemed from the same era as her automobile. When she saw me, she let out a wolf whistle and honked twice on a hand horn that was attached to the dashboard.

"Hey, you work here?" she asked.

"Yuh," I was stunned that she spoke to me.

"Well for Pete's sake, give me a hand." She jumped out the door, grabbed an armful of clothes, walked over and pushed them into my arms. "I'm going to be your next-door neighbor. Aren't you lucky?" She didn't wait for an answer but kept right on talking. "I'm Connie and I'm going to work as a seamstress for the Madam there in the dress shop. She's going to be mad as hell because I'm three days late, but I had to drive this joker to Camp Edwards. You gotta live for today! Grab those things and then get out of the way when the Madam starts to scream. What's your name?"

I was tongue-tied. I'd never seen anybody like her. I barely managed to get out, "Alan."

"I think you're too young for me," she replied as if she were thinking it over, "but that depends on what the other options are. We'll talk about it later." She made two clicking noises with her teeth and pointed to her automobile. "You think the 'Leaping Lizzie' is safe here?"

"Sure," I said.

"Isn't she beautiful?" she looked admiringly at the antique. "I just bought her very cheap. Now, take me to the front door of the shop and clear out of the line of battle."

I helped her with all her things and went back to setting my baskets. I could just about make out her apology for being late when the door slammed. I couldn't hear anymore.

Some days later, I got to talk to Mrs. Goodell, but we only exchanged a few words. Everybody called her Mrs. G. She barely spoke to the girls or anyone else. She was very haughty, and she lumbered around when she moved. She wasn't exactly fat, but her body was very unattractive. Liz, a good-looking brunette in her thirties, had arrived to help Mrs. G. sell the dresses and, of course, Connie was there.

During one of her cigarette breaks behind the store, Connie told me that the man named Jim was Mrs. G.'s lover and he was a drunk. Connie said all Mrs. G. did was order Jim around, and he drank to get the courage to stand up to her. At last, I thought Connie would be somebody I could spend time with. But when I asked her about going to the beach on Sunday, she said she was busy getting the lay of the land so she couldn't. She said maybe she'd be free the following week.

One day, I thought I had a great idea to get everyone together so that I'd have some friends for the summer. The four shops shared a back area that we used for garbage cans and empty packing cases that had arrived with merchandise. Some trees hung over it, so it was shaded from the sun. I found two wooden horses in the debris and a big piece of plywood. I lugged them out and made a table. I told Nana what I was doing, and she immediately said, "Don't think you're getting a penny from me for such foolishness. I don't want to be with those people."

I had saved a little money from selling cookies door to door in Brookline, so I bought some sandwiches and Cokes and invited Mrs. G., Jim and the girls to lunch. They all seemed to hesitate and said they didn't have much time. But I insisted that they didn't have to be there any longer than they wanted to be.

When they came out of the back door of their shop, I realized there was no place to sit. Jim helped me drag some of the folding chairs that they used when they did shows with their dresses, and we put them around my table. We all sat down, but nobody spoke. The girls just ate their sandwiches and Mrs. G. didn't speak to anybody, not even to Jim. I talked about the weather and how perfect Falmouth was, but no one responded.

Finally, Mrs. G. turned to me. "Do you go to church, Alan?" she asked.

I was stunned. It was so out of left field. No one had ever asked me that, or what religion I was. Finally, I said, "Well, no."

"You come with me some Sunday to the Christian Science church," she said. "You don't have to be a Christian Scientist. You'll see how much you like it."

I didn't want to make a big deal out of not being a Christian, so I just said, "Thank you. That would be nice." I figured she'd forget about it. I couldn't go into a Christian church. It wouldn't be right.

Everybody got up as soon as they could, thanked me, and went back to work. I threw the paper plates and cups into the trash and took the table apart. I knew it would never be used again.

Chapter 6

Sitting at the Inn every night for dinner with my grandmother and seeing all those old people at the other tables depressed me. Mrs. Hotchkiss didn't make it any better. Her maniacal laugh and her constant put down of her son Eddie made me wonder why any grown person would tolerate it. I had to put up with my grandmother, but I wasn't old enough to do anything else. I looked forward to the day when I finally would be. After dinner I would go back to the house and my dreary room. I tried to read, but the landlady kept a very weak bulb in the lamp. When I told her that I was bringing a stronger one to replace it, she said it would make the electric bill too high and she'd have to raise the rent. I knew Nana would never agree to that, so I just read until my eyes gave out.

My only escape was my diary and my photographs. Sometimes I would take off all my clothes and stand where the headlights of the oncoming cars would hit me. I wanted to cry out, "Look at me! I'm somebody you would like to know!" The drivers couldn't see me, but it made me feel alive for a moment.

Then in the morning, everything changed. Once I had a shower, put on a newly washed shirt, some pressed slacks, and combed my hair carefully, I was a different person. Maybe this would be the day something wonderful would happen. I raced my bike to the shop, opened up and began my routine setting up the baskets in neat rows on the sidewalk like a Mexican market. The sun was on the other side of the Byway, so it was cool and dark. The baskets gave off the sweet smell of newly mown grass and scented the fresh, clean air.

I stopped to watch the cars go by. I recognized some of the local people on their way to work in the center of town. Several cars that were obviously full of tourists slowed down to look at the signs to

Woods Hole and the beach. Then a convertible came by overflowing with rich kids from Buzzards Bay. They must be on their way to the town beach. I thought of yelling out to them and asking if I could hitch a ride, but they were too busy laughing and punching each other to even notice me.

When the cars let up for a few minutes, I saw a blond young guy sweeping in front of the newly opened men's store across the street. He was probably only a couple of years older than me, but he looked very grown up. He was wearing white flannels, a yellow pullover shirt and what I had wanted so much (but my parents wouldn't buy me) white and brown saddle shoes. He even had a crew cut. I kept looking at him. He reminded me of a cheerleader at a football game. He must have felt himself being watched because he looked up and saw me.

"Morning," he yelled.

"Morning," I replied.

He leaned the broom against the front of his store, walked across the street, and came over to me. He had a cocky, sure-of-himself stride. "You work here?" he asked.

"Yuh," I said trying not to seem too excited about this older boy stopping to talk to me.

"I'm Dudley," he said.

"I'm Alan."

Dudley put out his hand and I shook it. His grip was really strong as if he was making an extra effort to not have a wishy-washy handshake. "Do you know any girls?" he asked.

Actually, several from my class at school were going to a girl's camp a few miles away. I'd wanted to see them, but it was too far to go on my bike. "I do," I said, "but they're in Silver Beach—"

He cut me off. "That's okay. I've got a car, so why don't you set up a double date for Saturday?"

"I'm not sure they can leave the camp at night."

Dudley was persistent, "Why don't you find out and let me know?"

"I'll call them tonight," I said.

"Good," Dudley said. He went back across the street and opened the door of his shop. He turned back and yelled, "Let me know," and then he closed the door.

I was puzzled. Dudley didn't seem a bit friendly, but he did want to double date with me. Maybe he'd change after he got to know me better. I sure needed a friend, so I thought I'd better make allowances for him and see what happened.

I called Nancy Williams that night. She wasn't my girlfriend, but we used to pal around at school a lot. Her family was rich, and she'd take me to her parents' mansion for lunch once in a while. She wasn't pretty—she was short and squat—but she was smart, and we discussed books and current events. She really was a jock and won silver and gold cups for tennis constantly. We had an understanding that there was nothing romantic between us. That seemed to suit us fine. When she finally came to the telephone, she was very excited to hear from me, but she said the girls weren't allowed to leave the camp.

"There is a dance here on Saturday night," Nancy said. "Why don't you come and bring your friend if you can find a way to get here?"

"Oh, okay," I told her, "my friend has a car. Just give me directions."

When I saw Dudley the next day and told him about it, he seemed very excited. "This place is a morgue," he said. "We'll liven it up!"

It was a beautiful night. The moon was almost full, and it was cool enough to wear a jacket and tie and not perspire too much. I was nervous about Dudley picking me up. I was embarrassed to be living in such a seedy rooming house, but Dudley didn't mention it, so I felt relieved. I slid in beside him and gave him the directions to the camp. There was something exciting in the air and the smoke from Dudley's cigarette made me feel almost lightheaded. After about twenty minutes, we turned off the main road and followed a driveway that wound through piney woods to a huge shingled house. It didn't look anything like a camp, but we could hear loud music, so we knew we were in the right place. We took turns looking in the rear-view mirror, straightening our ties and checking out our hair. I combed mine but Dudley's was so short he only had to run his hand through it to make it stand up like the bristles on a brush.

We knocked on the front door, but when no one came, we figured they couldn't hear us with the music, so I tried the door and it was open. We walked into this huge living room, almost like a barn, with a beamed ceiling and an enormous stone fireplace. The wicker furniture was all stacked up and pushed close to the wall along with the rugs that had been rolled up. There must have been about thirty kids dancing to a record player, most of them girls and maybe half dozen boys. The house was perched on a cliff high above the ocean. Through the French doors at the far end of the room, I could see a streak of yellowish white that must have been coming from the moon reflecting on the dark sea below. As we stood there watching the dancers, Nancy spotted us and came rushing over. I'd forgotten how unattractive she really was. I now saw her as Dudley must be seeing her. She was wearing a plaid skirt with a big safety pin stuck into it. All the girls were wearing them, but it made her look even shorter and with her gray over-sized sweater she looked almost square. I introduced her to Dudley.

She said, "I have just the girl for you, Dudley." She ran over to where some girls were sitting out the dance and returned with a plain-looking one who had pimples covered with white cream that made them stick out even more. We split up and began to dance.

Nancy wasn't a good dancer, so she talked through the music as if to cover up her bad moves. The top of her head only came to my chest, so I had to bend over to hear her. "I had this terrible sumac poisoning," she said, "but since I was entered in the Cape Cod Championship, I couldn't very well back out of it." I threw her out in a jitterbug step, but as soon as I pulled her back, she went right on talking. "So, I went to Wianno and, you won't believe this, I won the singles, doubles, and mixed doubles, and I came back with three beautiful silver cups." She kept talking and talking, and I kept nodding and pushing her around like she was a ton of bricks.

The record player changed automatically and romantic numbers like "Between a Kiss and a Sigh," "I'm Waiting for Ships That Never Come In," and "Be Careful It's My Heart" played so I couldn't jitterbug to them. I had to hold Nancy close, but I was careful not to touch my body to hers below the waist. Not that I was attracted to her, but when I danced with Ronnie Markson, who I took to the Junior Prom, she pressed her body right against me, and I had to try like crazy not to get a hard-on. I didn't know what to do. I thought Ronnie would get angry if she felt it so I kept as far away as I could. Now I wasn't going to take any chances with Nancy.

The dances seemed interminable and my shoulders ached from trying to move Nancy around. I looked for Dudley and saw him dancing close to a very pretty girl who was laughing a lot. He must have gotten rid of the one with the pimples. The record player threw the records one by one, into a receptacle, but now that they had all played out, a girl went to turn the stack over. Dudley suddenly appeared. "I've got to go," he said.

Nancy protested, "We haven't had refreshments yet."

"I gotta work tomorrow," he said.

"But it's Sunday," she replied, "nobody works on Sunday. Besides, there are more girls I want you to meet."

"Sorry," Dudley said, "I have to do an inventory. Some other time."

We said our goodnights and walked outside to the car. We got in and Dudley took hold of the steering wheel without starting the car. I figured he'd had a lousy time, so I didn't say anything. I just waited for him to speak, but he just stared straight ahead. I felt these funny kinds of waves from him. I thought maybe he was angry because he wouldn't look at me. Finally, he did start up the car and when we'd driven well away from the house, Dudley pulled over. "I gotta pee," he said.

I got out with him, and we both walked across the road over to the edge of the woods. I felt I should say something, but I didn't know what. Dudley peed, making a loud sound as his stream hit the ground. I suddenly felt hot in the muggy air and my pee wouldn't come. I'd always had trouble peeing next to another guy, and I avoided it in school if I could. I'd wait until I was alone or try to find an empty stall. I figured Dudley would think I was peculiar if I didn't pee, so I tried desperately to think of warm water. I could feel Dudley looking at me, and I began to get excited as if there were something going on, something I was supposed to do, but I didn't know what it was. I became aware of the noises in the woods from all the insects, birds, and tree frogs. I could hardly breathe and suddenly Dudley broke his silence.

"Those girls were Jewish, weren't they?" he said.

For a moment I thought of lying. "Yes," I answered.

We got back into the car and Dudley drove me back to my room. Neither of us spoke until I got out of the car. "Night," I said.

"Night," he replied, and he zoomed down the highway.

Chapter 7

All these years later, I still remember that night going up to my room, undressing quickly, going out to the hall bathroom, brushing my teeth, returning to my room, locking the door, and getting into bed. I was glad to be by myself. I had to figure out what had happened. Why did Dudley ask me if the girls were Jewish? And why did he do that after, I'm sure, he was staring at me for so long? He must have seen that I was circumcised. Did that bring out his question? I wondered if he was an anti-Semite. There was so much of that going around. My family got letters from people in Germany who said they were related to us and wanted help to get to America because of the Nazis and the anti-Semitism there. So far, we hadn't known any of the people who wrote us, but it was getting to be a problem in the United States as well.

But I didn't think that was what it was. It wasn't just my imagination, but I had the feeling Dudley was waiting for something, something I was supposed to do. And then I started to remember what had happened that spring. As I lay there, I went over the whole incident. Maybe that would somehow give me the answer.

It was around the middle of March, but the weather was still cold and damp. The weekend was coming up and I didn't know what I was going to do with myself. One night the phone rang, and it was for me. Lenny Myers was in my class at school, but we weren't particularly friendly. Lenny was into athletics and on the football team, so we didn't have much in common.

"What are you doing this weekend?" Lenny asked.

"I don't know. I guess nothing," I said.

"My dad and I are going up to Maine to open the camp," Lenny replied, "and we thought you might want to go along."

I knew that Mr. Myers ran a camp for boys in the summer, but I'd never been there. "Sure," I said, "I'd like to, but I don't know if my parents will let me."

"Well, why don't you ask them and let me know. We're going to do some painting and stuff but nothing strenuous. You don't have to help out if you don't want to."

"No, I'd like to," I said, "it just depends on my parents and whether they've made any plans."

"Well, let me know." Lenny hung up.

I wondered why he had asked me and then it came to me. They must think if I see the place, I'll want to go there this summer. Anyway, it was something to do. I knew my parents would let me go.

After school on Friday, I waited for Lenny and his father to pick me up. Lenny had said to just bring some old clothes because we wouldn't be seeing anyone, and a bathing suit in case it warmed up. I threw one into the duffel bag, but I wasn't going to go swimming in a freezing lake. The doorbell rang and I ran downstairs. Lenny and his father were sitting in a beat-up station wagon filled with cardboard boxes. They helped me squeeze into the back between the cartons. Mr. Myers was a handsome, intellectual-looking man with rimless glasses and prematurely gray hair. He asked me questions about school as we pulled away from the curb, but the car was so noisy that we stopped talking after a few minutes.

Daylight savings had just taken place, but it was still pitch dark by the time we arrived at the sign that said "Camp Emoh for Boys." Lenny had told me Emoh was "home" spelled backwards. Mr. Myers said, "This is going to be one of your first tasks, Lenny, to repaint the sign."

Lenny didn't say anything as we turned into a long dirt road. The headlights reflected the water in the potholes from a recent rain. I couldn't see anything beyond the edge of the trees, until we came to a clearing where I could make out some cabins and a big building that must have been the dining room. I figured the lake must be somewhere between the trees, but it was too dark to see anything. We stopped and Mr. Myers unlocked one of the cabins and went in. A second later, we heard him say, "God dammit," and he came running out, furious. "I called them to be sure they put on the electricity and it's not working. These bloody people."

Mr. Myers positioned the car so that the lights shone through the open door and we could see to unload everything. We also found some candles inside that we lit with the matches Mr. Myers had for his pipe. The cabin was a mess with boxes on the floor, mattresses with no bedding, and torn-up paper and nutshells where an animal must have gotten in. The windows were covered with screening but no glass, only over-sized shutters to keep out the cold. Mr. Myers pushed up one shutter and propped it open with a stick. The chill of the air was unpleasant, but it cleared the mustiness from the room. We found sheets, blankets, and pillows in a cupboard, and we each made up our own bed. There wasn't any point of lighting up the gas stove in the main building because we wouldn't be able to see anything. We had sandwiches, so we sat on our beds and washed the food down with warm Cokes. Afterward, the three of us went outside and peed against the building. Without electricity there was no water, so we went to bed without washing or brushing our teeth. "One night won't hurt us," Mr. Myers said. "We'll have water in the morning."

I kept my shirt and sweater on, but I hung my pants over a chair. I felt awkward with Lenny and his father and I wondered whether I should have come. I piled blankets on my bed and got in. I listened to an owl hooting in the direction of where Lenny had said the lake was, and then I was fast asleep.

In the morning everything was better. The electricity had been turned on and there was water. Lenny and I took turns showering in the cubicle that had a cement floor covered with wooden slats, so you didn't have to stand in water. After we dressed and had breakfast, Mr. Myers gave us brushes and cans of green paint and we started on the dining room chairs. The day passed slowly. Lenny and I made small talk, but we didn't have much in common so most of the time we just painted. We stopped for lunch and then Lenny suggested we take a walk in the woods, but it started to rain before we could set out, so we went back to painting.

At the end of the day, there were still dozens of chairs unpainted, but Mr. Myers arrived and clapped us on the back and said how pleased he was with our work. He'd gotten some food in town that he heated on the stove. It didn't have any taste, but I ate it all to show I wasn't finicky. The steady drip of rain on the tar roof put me right to sleep, but when I woke in the night, I could feel the damp sheets against my body.

In the morning Mr. Myers said he had to spend the day in town seeing workmen about repairs. "You'll be on your own," he said to us, "so take a little time off. Why don't you get out one of the rowboats and go out on the lake? It's gotten warmer and it's going to be a beautiful day."

We had breakfast after he left and then I helped Lenny clean up. We tossed a coin to see who would shower first and I won. Afterward, I dressed while Lenny took his shower. The cabin was still a mess. Boxes and blankets and upturned chairs were everywhere. I saw a box marked "Athletic Equipment" and I opened it to find several football uniforms. I took out some shoulder guards and managed to get them settled around my neck. I rummaged through the box and found a jock strap and a hard, brown, curved shield about the size of my hand. I was holding it when Lenny came in with a towel around his waist. Lenny was stocky and not good-looking when he was dressed, but without his clothes, his body was athletic and well-defined.

"What are you doing?" Lenny asked.

I charged at him with the shoulder pads and we began to wrestle. Lenny was much stronger than I was, but he was being careful not to hurt me. We rolled around on the floor until Lenny held me down. I was still holding the shield in one hand. "What's this?" I asked panting for breath.

Lenny's eyes narrowed. "You know what it is."

"No, I don't," I said.

"It's a cup," Lenny said, "it goes over your cock to protect you."

I put it over Lenny's crotch, and he pushed it away, but I put it back again. "You horny bastard," Lenny said. I caught my breath and looked straight into Lenny's eyes. Lenny looked at me intensely and then, as if to break the tension, he grabbed me and started to wrestle again. I pushed the cup back over Lenny's crotch and again Lenny pushed it away. Several times I touched his penis by accident, and it started to get bigger. Lenny suddenly got up, grabbed the towel from where it had fallen on the floor, and held it in front of his erection. "Let's get out of here," he said.

I could hardly breathe. I followed Lenny, who was pulling on his clothes. We walked down to the lake. The sun was shining through the clouds and the water shimmered. Lenny opened the boathouse, and I helped him pull a rowboat down to the water's edge. He went back for oars and oarlocks and we pushed off into the lake. I was facing him as he rowed, and I could see that his penis looked like it would burst right through his pants. Lenny kept looking all around the lake as if he were afraid someone would see us. Mr. Myers had said no one lived there so I didn't understand why he was so worried. I found myself getting excited, too.

Lenny found an entrance to a small river on the other side of the lake and guided the boat into it until we couldn't see the camp any longer. I began to shake. The sun was fully out now, and it was quite warm, but I couldn't stop my teeth from chattering. Lenny suddenly pulled hard on the oars and the boat surged up onto the sand. We both got out. Neither of us said a word nor did we look at each other. Lenny took off his pants with difficulty. His penis was sticking out, and he had to take hold of it to get his clothes off. I took off my pants and underwear and we both kicked off our shoes. "Lie down on your belly," Lenny said huskily.

I lay down on the sand. It hurt my skin, but I didn't want to say anything and stop what was happening. Lenny lay on top of me and pushed up and down a few times. He must have been as uncomfortable as I was because he quickly stopped and stood up. I sat up and took Lenny's penis in my hand.

"Stop," he said and pulled me to my feet. We both looked around carefully. All we could see was the river sparkling in the sun and the tall beach grass waving in the wind. Lenny walked into the water up to his knees and stood there. He looked at me and I followed him in, not even feeling the cold. I took hold of Lenny and started to pull him. Lenny reached out for me and pulled me too. We forgot all about watching to see if anyone was around as we concentrated on each other. Lenny began to pant: "Oh, oh, oh" came from his throat rhythmically as if his heart was beating out the sounds. A spurt of liquid filled my hand and I began to come into the river. It was unlike any time I had masturbated. I just kept coming and coming. As the passion subsided and I came back to earth, I worried that I had broken something. I had never come for so long before, but finally, it stopped.

Now that it was over, we avoided each other's eyes. We washed ourselves off in the river and put our clothes back on. I felt ashamed and depressed as Lenny rowed us back to the camp. I was sure he felt the same way. I took a shower as soon as we got there, and I longed to get home and away from him. I could tell that he hated the sight of me, and he avoided me until Mr. Myers returned and we loaded the car. As we drove home, we pretended to be friendly in front of Mr. Myers, but it was clear we wouldn't see each other again.

I lay in bed mulling over the whole incident. Was that at all like the feeling I got coming from Dudley in the car and again as we stood at the edge of the woods together? Was that what he wanted? I wondered if I should ask him what it was that made him turn off me? Was it the Jewish thing, or was he waiting for me to do something?

On Monday, when I got to work, I saw Dudley across the street sweeping the sidewalk. When he saw me, he nodded and went inside his store. The next few days I saw him occasionally through the shop's plate glass windows, but he never came out. Finally, by the end of the week, I made up my mind to go over and have it out with him. What had I done? Why couldn't we be friends?

I opened the screen door of the men's shop and went in. There was a delicious smell of aftershave lotion and tables of cashmere sweaters in many colors. The whole place looked expensive. I felt grubby, like I didn't belong there. A man with a big chest, who looked like a football player, came from the back when he heard the door close. He was wearing white saddle shoes just like Dudley's.

"Is Dudley here?" I asked.

The man looked at me for a moment before he answered. "Dudley doesn't work here any longer. He's gone back to Boston."

"Thanks," I said. I went back across the street. I decided to try and forget the whole incident, but there was something mysterious about it. I wished I had a friend to talk to. Maybe somebody older who could explain it to me. But I didn't.

Chapter 8

One day, it was hot in the store. My grandmother had gone to the bank, so I was all by myself, dusting and rearranging merchandise. I was trying to make up my mind whether I should bike all the way to the little beach I had discovered on the way to Woods Hole or go to the pond that was behind the barbershop in town, sit near the old ice house, and read. These were my two favorite places to go to during my lunch hour, and neither was that exciting, but I had to get away from my grandmother and the shop for a while.

The wind chimes I had tacked onto the screen door tinkled, and I put down my dust rag. A woman in her sixties, who came into the shop often, called out, "Anybody here?"

I realized it was quite dark inside for someone coming out of the sun, so I walked toward her until she could see me. "Hello," I said.

"Oh, I didn't see you," she replied, "is your grandmother here?"

"No, but can I help you?" She was looking for a present for her nephew, and I walked around suggesting cigarette boxes, a Cape Cod barometer, or a leather desk set.

"You're a very clever young man," she said. "How old are you?"

"Fifteen," I told her.

"Well, you're certainly nice to help out your grandmother," she continued, "but you've got to get out and get some fresh air."

"Oh, I swim every day during my lunch hour."

"I think I'll take the barometer," the old woman said. "You should be with young people your own age." I began to wrap her purchase in gift paper. Luckily, I knew the price, so I didn't need Nana this time. "Why don't you come to my house one day for lunch and swim on my little beach? Would you like that?"

It was more of a command, than a question. I immediately answered, "Very much."

"Next Tuesday," she said, "I'll call for you at twelve-thirty."

"Thank you," I said hesitatingly, "but I can come on my bike."

"Nonsense. It's much too far." She swept out.

I went to the door and saw her get into a four-door open-sided, canvas-topped automobile that looked ancient but very expensive. She reached over the seat to a white, mannish hat that she picked up and pulled tight over her gray hair. She saw me watching her.

"Tell your grandmother Mrs. Hudson was here and that you're coming to lunch on Tuesday." She fumbled with the ignition until it took hold, and off she went without another word.

That night I wrote in my diary:

A wonderful old woman came into the shop today and asked me to go to her house for lunch. Nana says she is very rich and from one of the best families. I was reminded of Miss Havisham in Great Expectations *and I'm very excited about going. Maybe she will take the same kind of interest in me as the woman did to the boy in the book. We shall see...It's now quarter past ten and I have to go to sleep if I want to become that perfect being that I am aiming through training to be. Telephoned Nancy Williams at Mrs. Paul's Camp today and wrote a letter to Irving L.*

I drew the T and circle symbol and turned off the light.

On Tuesday, when I was in the car with Mrs. Hudson, I had second thoughts about going to her house. I didn't know what to say to her, and she made no attempt at conversation. She drove thirty miles an hour with that white hat on her head, and the breeze from the open window made the sailor collar on her sleeveless linen dress flap up and down. The heat from the noon sun came right through the canvas top and I had to sit up very straight to keep from falling asleep. When we had passed Silver Beach, Mrs. Hudson said, "It's not far now. I'm right on Buzzards Bay and I know you'll like it." I thought that was all she was going to say but she went on, "I live there all alone now, but I'm never lonely. My grandchildren come and visit, and I always have the gulls and the sea. I consider myself fortunate."

I didn't know what to say to that, but she didn't seem to want me to say anything. We followed a road that hugged the cliff and looked down at the Bay. There were sailboats out on the horizon and the sea was sapphire colored as it reflected the cloudless sky. We finally stopped at a house at the very edge of the cliff. Only the upper story was visible from the road. When we went inside, I saw a staircase that led down to a living room that seemed to be suspended above the water. Since the sun was directly overhead, only a slice of it shone through a window and created a bit of light on the dark wood floor.

In the slice of sun sat a huge, molasses tabby cat luxuriating in the warmth. There were bookcases everywhere and club chairs covered in flowered chintz. Reading lamps were by each chair and a huge comfortable-looking sofa faced the view. There was a feeling of peace and serenity I'd never experienced in a house before. Our apartment in Brookline certainly didn't have it. The closest I'd ever come to feeling like that was when I babysat once in a really beautiful house. The kids were asleep, and I sat alone in a nice living room in a wing chair by the fireplace, doing my homework. It was so still, and I felt so safe. I remember thinking that was the way I was going to live someday.

Mrs. Hudson gave me a towel, showed me where to change, and pointed out the path to the sea. There must have been a hundred stone steps I had to go down to get to a small cove where I could swim. It seemed like the Riviera that I'd seen in the movies, and I daydreamed that Mrs. Hudson would ask me to live there forever.

When I got back up to the house, there was a plate with two sandwiches and a glass of milk waiting for me. The old woman said she didn't eat lunch, but she watched as I ate. She asked me questions about my parents and my school that I answered, but there were many moments when neither of us said anything. I just stared out at the sea and listened to the ticking of the grandfather clock. As soon as I finished eating, Mrs. Hudson stood up.

"Well, I have to get you back," she said. "Your grandmother will be wondering what happened to you."

"Oh, that's all right," I said trying to prolong the experience, "there's no hurry."

Mrs. Hudson was already gathering her bag and her white hat, and she ushered me up the stairs to the car. There was no further conversation on the drive back. I suddenly had the feeling that I'd been treated like a poor child taken for an outing at the beach by a rich lady who felt sorry for me.

Mrs. Hudson didn't come into the shop again for the rest of the summer. Nana asked me if I'd said anything rude to her or done something wrong. I said of course not, but I wondered what I had done. The only thing I figured was that I just didn't measure up. But what was it that I didn't measure up to? I didn't know.

Chapter 9

As the summer went by, most days were the same. I worked in the shop waiting on customers, that is if there were any. My grandmother usually grabbed anybody who opened the door, and I only got someone if there was more than one person. I did pretty well, though, and managed to sell a lot. Nana never thanked me, but I was used to that. After the lunch at Mrs. Hudson's, I felt kind of gloomy. I did get away at lunchtime for a swim and to read one of my books at the beach. I had bought a few Modern Library books of plays by Clifford Odets and Eugene O'Neill. I secretly wanted to be an actor, but I'd never told anyone. I just wasn't sure I was good-looking enough. I'd always gotten a lot of compliments on my looks as I grew up and I once even entered my picture in "The Most Beautiful Child" contest when I was ten, but I didn't win.

I was beginning to feel more and more insecure. I tried to talk to my grandmother about it since there was really nobody else that I was even close to, but she was always preoccupied selling in the store or reading her romance novels. When we had dinner at Mrs. Hotchkiss', she was so busy slurping her food and running her tongue over her false teeth that I couldn't even look at her, let alone talk to her. One night I rode my bike until I caught up with her walking to the rooming house. I got off the bike and pushed it alongside her.

"I want to ask you something," I said as we walked.

"Vot?" she said suspiciously. (Her accent was especially noticeable in "w" words.)

"Well, it's kind of a difficult thing to say."

"You vant to go home?" she stopped and looked at me.

I stopped too. "No, I'll stay 'til Labor Day, the way we arranged it."

"Vell, vat is it?"

"Am I good-looking?" I asked sheepishly.

"Vat do you vant to know that for?"

"I just do," I said. "Am I?"

"Och," she made a funny sound. "You're all right."

"That's not an answer." I said. "Am I?"

"Your nose is too big," she replied and walked on.

I got back on my bike and arrived at the rooming house before she did. I rushed to the bathroom and looked in the mirror. I turned my face in different ways, but I couldn't see my nose at every angle. I went to my room and locked the door. I couldn't bring myself to put what she said in my diary. I just went to bed and tried to forget it, but I couldn't.

The summer was going fast, and I still didn't have any friends. I never got to know any of the kids in town because I was always working in the shop. I didn't know how to go about meeting them. The rich kids who lived in the Heights had their own cliques, and even at the beach they didn't mix with anybody else. Mrs. Goodell always said "Hello," and "We've got to have that talk one of these days" but we never did, and Jim was always hung over.

The two girls at the candy store were locals and I went in to talk with them once in a while, but they were in their twenties. They teased me and fed me chocolates and once dared me to eat one of each of the twenty-one different candies the store sold. I did it, but it turned me off chocolates for weeks. I thought Connie and I were going to be friends, but she was always running out of the store to go somewhere or arriving too late for work to stop and talk. One day I managed to grab her before she got into the Leaping Lizzie.

"Connie," I yelled, "what about the beach this Sunday?"

She stopped and came over to me. "I'm sorry," she said, "I haven't had a chance to tell you. The Leaping Lizzie broke down and I took it into this garage. There was this gorgeous guy who fixed it and asked me for a date. It's been a whirlwind. We're together every minute when we're not working. He's a fireman. I think he's going to ask me to marry him, and boy, will I. I'm sorry not to spend time with you. You're a really nice kid."

Connie reached out to pat me on the shoulder and something fell out of her purse. I picked it up for her. It was a thin tin box with R and L in large letters on the front. "What is this?" I asked. "Is it medicine? Are you sick?"

She looked at me for a minute. "Don't you know?" I shook my head. "R and L stands for rubber and lubricant."

"Oh sure," I said pretending I knew, but I'd never heard about it before.

"Well I gotta run." She zoomed off and several weeks later did find time to tell me he had "popped the question." She was gone from Mrs. Goodell's within a week, and I didn't even see her riding around town anymore. She told me before she left that Lester, her "beau" she called him, wanted her to be "a hellion at home and an angel in church," and she was going to fit the bill.

I'm sure she did.

Chapter 10

After Connie left, Mrs. Goodell seemed to be at her store more often. I imagine she had to do some of the alterations Connie had done. As a result, I bumped into her occasionally, and one day she told me that she was going to church on Sunday and asked if I would like to go along.

"Oh, I don't really want to go to church," I said nervously. "Maybe some other time."

"You don't have to go inside the church if you don't want to, but it's a lovely ride and we'll have a picnic. I'll make some sandwiches. It'll do you good to get away from here."

I never had anything to do on Sunday, so I finally said yes. I just had to be with some people for a change. It would be a treat even though they were so much older. They might turn out to be friends.

It was a July day at its best, feeling more like a perfect day in June. Soft miniature clouds hid the sun, but only for a second now and then. A fresh breeze rustled the heavy leaves drooping from the trees and the summer seemed to be standing still, holding its breath. I was in the backseat of Mrs. Goodell's car. I tried to ignore her and Jim bickering as we drove out of Falmouth. I wondered why they were always fighting. They weren't married, so if they didn't like each other, why didn't they just separate? Jim was driving, and Mrs. Goodell had to turn around as far as she could to say something to me.

"You don't have to come into the church if you don't want to," she said," but I think it would do you a world of good."

"No, thank you," I replied, "I just don't feel right about it."

"Alan," she coaxed, "don't be absurd. I know what's bothering you.

Lots of Jewish people are Christian Scientists. You won't feel uncomfortable."

"I just think I'd better not." In school when we sang Christmas carols, I could never sing "Jesus" or "Christ" out loud because I was afraid it was a sin, so how could I go into a Christian church?

"Leave him alone," Jim interjected irritably. "He can wait in the car with me." I could tell that Jim was really hung over, and the prospect of sitting with him alone wasn't so great. "Don't try to get everyone to do what you want them to do," Jim said as if he was ready to start up their fight again.

Mrs. Goodell jumped right down his throat, "It wouldn't do you any harm to go to church either. There's a lot it could do for you, but I'm not going to waste my breath. I've tried long and hard enough." She stopped talking and sat facing straight ahead as if that could separate her from Jim.

We pulled up in front of a long shed painted white with a small cupola over the double doors that marked the entrance. Mrs. Goodell put on a hat and attached it to her hair with a long bobby pin. "I'll be about an hour," she said. "You two, behave."

I hadn't realized she'd be gone that long and I knew it would be agony talking to Jim, so I said, "No, I'll come with you."

"Good," she said with a triumphant look at Jim, and she took my arm and led me towards the church.

The inside of the building was very plain. There were about fifty folding chairs facing a slightly raised platform that had a simple wooden chair and a table. It looked like a meeting hall that had been painted white. There was no color except for two bouquets of flowers on either side of the dais—blue delphiniums, orange black-eyed Susans, white baby's breath and pink yarrow—all flowers I knew from my Aunt Rae's garden when I was growing up on the Cape. They stood out so against the stark-white setting.

The two of us sat beneath an open window with the sun pouring in and spotlighting the flowers. I felt very peaceful and listened to the simple sermon, so different from the ones I'd heard when

I went to temple with my parents. There was nothing formal or uncomfortable about it. It just seemed like ordinary life. It certainly wasn't mysterious. I put aside my fears and thought, "It's all right. God will understand."

As we were driving back to Falmouth after we'd had our sandwiches on the side of the road, Mrs. Goodell suddenly put her hand on Jim's arm. "This is Truro," she said, "isn't it?"

"Yuh, I think so," Jim answered.

"It's where Juddie lives," she said. "Let's go see him."

"You can't go barging in on someone without any notice," he said.

"I'm dying to see his house," she replied with relish, "and he told me to come by whenever I was in the neighborhood."

Jim lowered his voice, "What about him?" he whispered and turned his head slightly toward me. I was being talked about, so I listened more carefully.

"What do you mean?" she asked.

"You know," Jim said with some kind of meaning I didn't understand.

"You really make me sick," Mrs. Goodell snorted. "What do you think he's going to do with us right there? I want to see that house!"

Jim took a few wrong turns, so it was ten minutes before we found the address Mrs. Goodell had in her little address book. We drove into a short driveway and discovered a perfectly restored Cape Cod cottage. It was covered in white clapboard and looked like the doorstops we sold in the shop, even to the hollyhocks blooming out front.

As we got out of the car, a plump man in his fifties spotted us. "Edith," he yelled, "what a delight." He came running up from a section of garden that curved around the side of the house and embraced her. He immediately stopped her saying she hoped she wasn't disturbing him. "I would have been furious if you hadn't come by," he said in the most perfect accent that almost sounded British. "I know you especially will appreciate this gem," he indicated the house with a slight hand gesture. Then he turned and yelled to a handsome young man in the garden who was teasing a pretty girl with a huge beach ball, "Behave yourselves, you two."

When we were in the house, I had to keep my mouth from dropping open. I'd never seen anything like it. He told us that he'd added several wings onto the original building as he took us from one beautiful room to another. The floors and all the antique furniture were highly polished, and although the ceilings were low, as I knew they were in early cottages, they still had the original beams that were gnarled with age. Hooked rugs with patterns of either flowers or animals were scattered over the floors. Oversized fireplaces filled with dried flowers dominated the tiny rooms. We climbed a staircase barely wide enough for us to get by, that took us to bedrooms with four-poster beds covered with comforters that matched the curtains.

"It's absolutely perfect," Mrs. Goodell said. "You've done it exquisitely. I've never seen anything like it."

Juddie's round face was flushed with pleasure. "Thank you, Edith," he said. "You can imagine what it's been like with these locals. They suggested taking up the random-width floors and putting in new ones."

Mrs. Goodell joined Juddie's laughter. "No," she screamed.

When we were downstairs again, he was particularly nice to me, encouraging me to ask questions about the implements in front of the fireplace that the colonials had used for cooking. He seemed to be having a good time showing us the house. There were little beads of perspiration on his forehead at the edge of his carefully combed silver hair, and his blue eyes sparkled with pleasure as he showed off his treasures.

The screen door suddenly burst open and the young man and the girl we'd seen in the garden walked in. He was only wearing a tiny bathing suit, and his muscular body was dark as a chestnut. The girl, who was overshadowed by his good looks, stood somewhat behind him.

"Oh good, you're here," Juddie said and introduced them, "This is my niece Ann, and this is Johnny Parks, who's staying with me." We all shook hands. "I was just telling young Alan here how our ancestors cooked," he said, giving Johnny a look; "and now we must all have some coffee." Johnny looked straight at him, ignoring us completely, and then ran out the door pulling the girl behind him. We could hear their laughter as they romped in the garden. There was a moment as the four of us just stood awkwardly not knowing what to say.

Mrs. Goodell finally broke the silence, "We really must be getting back."

"Well," Juddie said not even trying to hide his annoyance with the young man, "perhaps it's just as well. We're late for lunch and you'll come another time. And do bring Alan again."

As we got into the car, I looked back at the house and saw the young man staring at me from the garden. I must have done something to annoy him, but I couldn't think what. I should think he'd be happy just staying in such a wonderful place surrounded by beautiful things and all those flowers. He seemed to have everything. *That's the way I'm going to live someday*, I thought to myself.

When we were some distance from the house, Mrs. Goodell said, "Well, that was certainly interesting."

Jim, who hadn't said a word the whole time we were there, replied, "Is that the one he calls his nephew?"

"You notice he didn't call him that in front of his niece," Mrs. Goodell said. And then, as if she remembered I was there, she turned around and asked if I had enjoyed seeing the house.

"Oh yes," I said, "and he was so nice to me."

"Um" was the only sound Mrs. Goodell made, and neither of them said anything more.

They dropped me off at the shop to get my bike. I thanked them, and they drove off. Something was funny. All that about the nephew, and why did he give me such a look as we were leaving? I had a feeling there was some mystery they wouldn't talk to me about. They treated me like I wasn't old enough to know. What was it? It made me a little depressed, but I was fascinated, too. Maybe I could ask Jim when Mrs. Goodell wasn't around.

Chapter 11

On my way to the shop all summer, I'd been passing a country store that was being turned into a place for antiques. Construction had begun last year. I knew the guy who had brought it down from New York state, so I was interested to see how much had been completed. One day I stopped in front of the store to get a good look. I stayed seated on my bicycle, balancing myself by putting my right foot down on the sidewalk. The building seemed so out of place, set down in the midst of the white-frame houses that lined the highway. Some of the townspeople had gossiped about it. They thought it ridiculous to spend money to bring a structure all the way from upstate New York that looked like an ordinary country store, even if it was built in 1820.

I examined it carefully. It wasn't ordinary. There was something strange about it, as if it came from another world. The shop was covered with brown, weathered wood. There was a pulley hanging over two doors in the upper story and two large shop windows on either side of a door in the lower one. At the entrance was a sign that read "Antiquarium." The landscape was finished now and extremely elaborate in contrast to the simplicity of the store. The semi-circular white pebble driveway surrounded by lush plantings made me think the building looked like an ordinary rock that had been placed in a ring of gold.

"Hi there." The voice startled me.

I saw Dave Garland watching me from the side of the building. I felt as if I'd been caught doing something wrong. "I was just admiring your store," I said guiltily.

"Wouldn't you like to see the inside?" Dave asked.

"Oh yes," I replied, excited at the prospect of seeing something everyone was talking about. I put down the kickstand on my bicycle and followed Dave inside. The morning was very hot, and it was a relief to walk into the cool darkness of the room. When my eyes adjusted, I saw what looked like a museum with elegant objects arranged on dark oak tables that reflected them in the waxed surfaces. There must have been a dozen chandeliers hanging from the high ceiling. Wherever I looked, I saw more treasures: decanters and glasses, ivory boxes, delicate chess sets, French sofas and chairs covered in intricate needlepoint, fine china—all things of great beauty. It was such a contrast to the plain outside that I felt like I'd stumbled into a lost Egyptian tomb.

Dave flipped a switch, and everything was bathed in the softest light that came from the tole lamps scattered throughout the room. The light was caught up in the hundreds of crystals on the chandeliers and sparkled like Christmas.

"How beautiful," I said. "I've been riding by every day on my way to work, but I had no idea it was anything like this."

"Come and see the garden," Dave said.

He took me through a door and into a large room where he obviously lived. Piles of dirty clothes surrounded an unmade bed and there were stacks of books on every spare inch of the floor. After the beauty of the store, it looked like a cheap hotel room.

"Don't mind the mess," he said. "I have so much to do in the store, I just don't get the time to clean in here."

Dave led me through the obstacle course of his bedroom. French doors opened onto a terrace. A lawn smooth as a putting green was surrounded on three sides by beds of flowers that edged the woods. A gardener was weeding, completing the picture that could have been on the cover of a magazine.

"I spend all my free time out here," Dave said. "Sit down for a minute."

I leaned against the back of a wrought-iron chaise and looked out at the woods. I breathed in the odor of the newly mown grass and the flowers. *This is the way I want to live*, I thought. *Like this or like Juddie's cottage. It's so peaceful and beautiful.*

"Are you helping your grandmother in her shop for the summer?" Dave asked.

"Yes. She's getting kind of old and my parents thought somebody should keep an eye on her."

I was pleased that he remembered who I was. I had often seen him in past summers when I was growing up. Then, he had had a small shop near my grandmother's on the Byway. I watched him come out of his store, all dressed up, and get behind the wheel of his station wagon. I was sure he was headed to some wonderful, exciting party. I'd wave to him and he'd wave back, but this was the first time he had ever talked to me. I looked at him sitting on the other chaise. He had always seemed so handsome from a distance, but up close, his features were not that great, and his eyes were lined with creases from the sun. He looked like he worked out a lot because his body was very muscular, almost too big for his small head. He did, however, have splendid black hair and a friendly smile.

"I hope you're not working too hard," Dave went on. "Are you getting any time to swim?"

"Oh yes," I said. "I take off every day at lunchtime and go to a little beach near Woods Hole."

"I know a beach near Woods Hole where you can swim without a suit at night. Maybe it's the same place. Would you like to come with me sometime?"

"Thank you," I said, "but I think I'd be too embarrassed."

"Why?" Dave asked. "We're just two men."

"I wouldn't want anyone to see my body yet. I'm just working on it, and it's not very good."

Dave laughed, "It looks fine to me. You could get those biceps a little larger." He reached over and pressed a finger into my upper arm like a gym instructor. He stood up. "Let's go back inside," he said.

We crossed through the bedroom again and went back into the store. On the way, Dave grabbed a book from a table. "Have you read this?" he asked.

I looked at the title: *Wind, Sand and Stars.* "Not yet," I said as if I read all the current best sellers.

"I think you'd enjoy it," he said. "An aviator wrote it."

"I'll get it at the lending library," I replied.

"No, I'm finished with it. You can borrow it."

"Thank you," I said as I took it from him. I was getting used to Dave's speech. At first, I thought it was affected, but I decided he must come from an upper-class Boston family. I was about to ask him if he did when he startled me.

"I'll bet you masturbate a lot," he said.

No one had ever said that word out loud to me. I tried to hide my astonishment. I guessed it must be a subject that men of the world discussed openly so I said, "Yuh, I suppose I do."

Dave pressed me further. "How often do you do it?"

"Well," I replied, "I try not to do it more than once a day. I make a mark in my diary so I can remember if I've done it or not. Sometimes I cheat and don't put down the mark so I can do it twice."

Dave walked over to the window and looked out. "There's nothing wrong with it," he said.

"Oh, I know," I said. "I know everybody masturbates." I said the word forcefully to show how grown up I was.

"Lower your voice," Dave said.

"Why?" I asked, surprised by his furtive tone.

"The gardener might hear us," Dave said. "You know the funny ideas these people can get."

I felt my heart beating too fast. There was something unspoken at that moment that I wanted to know. It was just like Jim whispering to Mrs. Goodell about the young man at Juddie's, or that funny episode with Dudley. Maybe Dave would tell me what it was.

I was trying to summon up the courage to ask him when he suddenly said, "Your grandmother must be wondering what happened to you, and I've got to get back to work."

I felt I'd done something wrong, but I didn't know what. His whole attitude toward me changed. He took me to the door. I thanked him for the book and said I would return it as soon as I read it. "No, no," he said. "You keep it. I have too many books as it is. And I'm so busy most of the time, I can't really see people."

I went over to my bicycle. I suddenly thought, *I'll go back and tell him I'll go swimming with him. Maybe then he'll tell me what all these secrets are about.* But the door was closed. I put the book in the basket of my bike. I had a feeling that whatever had happened, Dave didn't want to see me again.

A few days later, I wrote in my diary:

I am reading a book that Dave Garland gave me. He showed me around his new antique store. He reads all the best new books. This one is the first really non-fiction novel that has no plot that I think I have ever read. I hope I'm graduated into adult reading now. It tells the philosophies and life of a French airmail pilot. One quotation I like very much follows: "We had met at last. Men travel side by side for years. Each locked up in his own silence. Then they stand shoulder to shoulder. They discover that they belong to the same family...Happiness. It is useless to seek it elsewhere than in the warmth of human relationships. Our sordid interests imprison us within their walls. Only a comrade can grasp us by the hand and haul us free." It's now quarter past ten and I have to go to sleep if I want to become that perfect being that I am aiming to be through training. Called Nancy Williams at Mrs. Paul's Camp today and wrote a long letter to Irving L.

I drew the T and circle symbol and turned out the light.

Chapter 12

My grandmother and I got to the store early. We were in the process of putting labels that said "Cape Cod, Mass." over all the merchandise that was stamped "Japan" on the bottom. The label fit perfectly and made it seem like whatever it was came from Cape Cod. There was a bad feeling about the Japanese at that time, so people didn't want to buy things from Japan. There were many in the shop because they were so cheap to buy, and the Japanese were so great at making good copies of things from other countries. I thought it was a lie making believe that something was made in Cape Cod when it wasn't, so if someone asked me where it was from, I told them the truth. But in the meantime, I had to do what my grandmother told me.

My life with her would, thankfully, be over soon. It was almost the end of August. I would be going back to Brookline right after Labor Day. I felt I had nothing to show for the summer. I hadn't made any friends or had much fun outside of going to the movies a few times. One picture I did see was called *All This and Heaven Too* with Bette Davis. I was really enjoying it when my grandmother ruined one of the best scenes by making noise rubbing her hands together. Everyone yelled, "Shush."

"Vhat's the matter?" she'd said loudly. "My hand's asleep." The audience laughed, but I was embarrassed. She had a way of spoiling everything.

As we worked with the labels, I decided to ask her for a gift. "I've worked very hard and I haven't been paid."

"Vhat d'ya mean?" she replied. "You got your room and board, don't you?"

"But I haven't got anything that says I was here, something to put in my room to look at and remember this summer."

"You're crazy. I don't know vhat you're talking about."

"I want you to give me something. Something I'll always remember."

"Vhat?" Nana asked me suspiciously.

I walked across the store to a long table covered with merchandise. I picked up a cut glass decanter and went back to her, holding it out in front of me. "This," I said.

"Vhat do you vant that for?"

"I want to put it in my penthouse when I move to New York," I said. And then I said it again as if repetition would make it come true. "I want to put it in my penthouse when I move to New York."

"That costs a lot of money," she said pointing at the decanter and pursing her lips. "You don't need it."

"Please, Nana. Promise me you'll give it to me if no one buys it before I leave."

"Vhat do you vant a thing like that for?" she asked, as if nothing I'd said had made any impression on her.

I decided I'd try to bargain with her. "What do you have to lose? You probably will sell it, and if you don't, you'll give it to me as a present. Either way, you'll win."

I'm not sure she could figure out whether this was a good deal or not, but she finally sighed, "All right. Now leave me alone."

I was elated. I figured since nobody had bought the decanter all summer, chances were that nothing would happen in the next couple of weeks. And if someone got interested, I would have to point out the scratch on the stopper. It was a sign. My dream of New York would come true one day.

Chapter 13

On Sundays, I usually went to a small beach near Woods Hole where I could be alone, read my book, and enjoy the quiet. It wasn't really a beach but more like a strip of sand, so nobody went there. It was so hot the last week in August. There wasn't even a trace of a cloud in the sky. I packed my towel and my Modern Library book of *The Plays of Eugene O'Neill* in the basket on my bike and took off. When I got to the fork that led either to Woods Hole or the Falmouth town beach, I changed my mind. I didn't have the energy to peddle all the way to Woods Hole, and I felt it might be nice to just have people around for a change. I turned left and rode out past the grand houses where the rich people lived.

At the ocean, beyond the dune grass, there was a stretch of sand that connected with the private beach but was still public. There was no lifeguard or float to swim out to, so it wasn't as populated as the main beach. I decided to spend the day where it would look like I'd chosen to be alone and yet I still could see other people. I put the lock on my bike and spread out my towel at some distance from the nearest group. I went into the water. The surf was strong, and I was having trouble walking out between waves. I was looking back toward shore when a wave hit me and knocked me over. I wasn't hurt, but my nose and ears filled with saltwater, so I clambered out and threw myself down to dry off.

I must have fallen asleep. When I looked around there were many more people on the beach. I sat up. Near me were two women, both around twenty, laughing with a handsome man who seemed older. His brown hair was tousled by the wind and his small ears stuck out slightly from his head. It added humor to his good looks. The man seemed to feel me looking at him and turned my way. For a moment, we both stared at each other and then the man went on talking to his companions. I picked up my book, but I couldn't concentrate. I kept looking back at the man who seemed to be having such a good time with his friends. They were laughing and enjoying each other so much that I felt more alone than ever.

Several times I met the man's gaze, but when I looked again, he was busy. I must have imagined it. One time, I turned to find him looking straight at me and he smiled. I quickly looked away to hide my face. I could feel it was flushed. When I turned back, the man ignored me. I began to hope the he would look at me again, but each time I got up the courage to face him, he was busy talking and looking the other way. I was feeling quite hot and thought that I was staring too much, so I forced myself to read my book. I was just getting into *Anna Christie* when I heard a voice say, "How's the book?"

I looked up. It was the man I had been staring at. I could see beyond him that the women he'd been with had left. "I've just begun reading it," I said. I was having trouble breathing and suddenly felt frightened, as if there were some danger.

"Can I sit down?" the man asked.

"Of course," I answered him. I smoothed out the large towel so there was room for both of us.

The man settled near me and put out his hand. "I'm Roger Alton," he said.

I shook his hand, but I avoided his eyes. "Alan Schein," I said. "I'm glad to know you." My chest felt constricted. I didn't know what to say, and yet I felt if I didn't say something, he would get up and leave.

"Want to go for a swim?" Roger asked.

"Sure," I said, and we both got up and walked into the sea.

The shock of the cold water seemed to relieve my tension and the two of us swam out together. The waves had subsided somewhat, so we were able to swim close to each other. When I stopped and treaded water, Roger stopped too. He had an amazing smile. I smiled back and everything seemed perfectly natural, as if we had known each other for a long time. We didn't speak, yet I suddenly felt relaxed. We left the water and walked back to my towel. I picked it up to dry myself, but first I shook out the sand.

"I'm afraid I only have this one," I said.

"Shall I bring my things over here?" Roger asked.

"Sure," I answered, and watched as Roger went over to his towel and gathered up his cigarettes, a book, and a blue parka with a hood. When we were settled, Roger lit a cigarette but didn't offer me one. I figured it was because he thought I was too young to smoke, and it bothered me. Roger nodded toward my book that still had its paper cover with "O'Neill" in big letters splashed across it.

"You like O'Neill?" he asked.

I had just read a few pages. "I think so," I answered. "I've always wanted to read him. Do you like him?"

"Yes and no," Roger said as he exhaled. "Some of it's a bit pretentious for me, but I think you'll enjoy it. Do you like the theater?"

"Yes, I want to be an actor." I realized it was the first time I'd ever said that to anyone. I held my breath. I expected Roger to say I was crazy, but instead he took it as a matter of course.

"I should think you'd do very well at it. You're good-looking enough," he said. "Have you ever acted?"

"Not really. I'm in the dramatic society at school and I won honorable mention at Prize Speaking this year."

"That's great," Roger said.

The smoke from his cigarette mingled with the salt air, and it smelled delicious to me. "There were six honorable mentions out of ten contestants," I confessed.

Roger smiled. "Still." We sat quietly for a few moments. Then he asked, "Where are you going to college?"

"I haven't made up my mind yet. I think I want to go to Dramatic School, but I haven't told my parents that. They're trying to force me to go to college."

"Oh, you're still in high school?"

I panicked at the thought of his not wanting to spend any more time with me if he knew how young I was. "I'm graduating this year," I said and quickly changed the subject. "Where did you go to college?"

"Mass State, but I don't think that would be good for you if you want to be an actor."

We fell into a pleasant conversation and I stopped being afraid I'd say the wrong thing. I relaxed enough to be totally myself. I always tried to act grown up with people older than me. But that made me kind of stiff. Roger somehow put me at my ease. I found out that he lived in Falmouth year-round and was a landscape architect. I told him about working for my grandmother on the Byway.

Roger lit another cigarette. "Oh, I'm sorry," he said, "would you like one?"

"No, thank you," I said, delighted that at least he thought I was old enough to smoke. I noticed that the beach was thinning out. The volleyball game had ended, and the woman who had been serving lemonade out of a huge Thermos jug to her children had packed her things and gone home. I didn't want the afternoon to end.

He got up and took his wristwatch out of the parka. "I'm afraid it's getting late. I'd better go."

"Want to go for a swim tomorrow?" I asked.

"I'm afraid I can only get away on weekends, but maybe we'll see each other on the beach next week."

I stood up. "Well, I guess I'd better be going too."

He turned to me. "You want me to drop you off? I have my car."

"That would be swell, but I've got my bike here."

"That's okay, it's a convertible. I'll put the top down and it can go in the backseat."

We took my bicycle over to a tan Ford. Roger put the top down and lifted the bike into the back. As we drove by the estates close to the water, he asked me if I had many friends in Falmouth.

"Just the people who work on the Byway," I said, "but they're usually pretty busy. Do you have a lot of friends?"

"Some, but I've lived here for a few years."

"Where do you live?"

"Pin Oak Way," he replied.

With the top down, I felt like one of the rich kids I always saw driving by the shop laughing and having fun. The breeze kept blowing the scent of Roger's aftershave in my direction.

"Your aftershave is terrific," I said. "What is it?"

Roger laughed. "I guess I put it on too heavily this morning. It's called Old Spice."

I didn't want him to see where I lived so I asked him to drop me at the store. We said goodbye and I kept hoping he would suggest our getting together again, but he just repeated what he had said before, about maybe seeing me on the beach next weekend. I watched his car drive away. All I could think of was that next weekend would be too late. It was Labor Day, and I would be going home. How could there be time enough for us to become friends?

Chapter 14

I didn't know what to do with myself the following week. I never stopped thinking about Roger. I wanted so much to be his friend, but I guess there wasn't much reason for him to be interested in me. *After all*, I thought, *I'm half his age and I work in a filthy gift shop for a sloppy old woman who even has an accent*. For several days, I just stood at the front of the store looking out the window, hoping he would come by. But all I saw were the maple trees, their leaves drooping from the rain.

When the sun finally came out, I rode around the town on my bicycle, going to all the places I thought I might run into him. He wasn't in the Five and Ten and he wasn't in the post office. He didn't seem to be anywhere. I even went over to Pin Oak Way where Roger said he lived. It was a dead-end street with nice houses set off behind green lawns and gardens bordered with trellised arbors. I rode up and down the street trying to figure out which house was his, but I didn't have the address. I kept hoping he would come out one of the doors, but when he didn't, I went back to the store.

Nana was reading one of her lending-library romances in the back room. I went over to the cash drawer. Very quietly I pressed the first and third keys under the drawer. The drawer flew open but I caught it with my hand so there wouldn't be any noise. I took out several dollars and shut the drawer quietly. I listened to see if Nana had heard anything but there was no sound behind the curtain.

"I'm going out for a few minutes," I yelled.

I got on my bike and rode over to the green where they had the county fair every July. Eighteenth century houses surrounded the old sheep meadow with its wrought-iron fences and tall elms. On one side were a few stores, and I leaned my bike against a low wall in front of the pharmacy. I felt a little guilty about taking money from Nana, but she certainly owed me for all my work. I had used up what little I'd saved on ice cream cones and an occasional movie, and I needed the two dollars I'd taken very badly.

I went inside and saw a woman buying something at the counter. I pretended to look through the postcards while I waited for her to finish. When she had left the store, I walked over to the old man who had just rung up the sale. I used my deepest voice.

"Have you got any Old Spice?" I asked, afraid that I would be challenged with, "What do you want that for? You're too young to shave."

Instead the man said, "Which kind?"

I got confused. "I don't know, just Old Spice."

"Well, we got cologne and we got aftershave."

"The aftershave is fine." I felt I was doing something that I shouldn't do, so I paid the dollar and a half the druggist asked for as soon as I could. I grabbed the cardboard box from his hand, refused a bag, and rushed out the door. I went over to a clump of bushes and stood behind them. When I was sure no one could see me, I opened the box and took out the ceramic bottle. I pulled off the metal top, closed my eyes, and inhaled deeply. It was just like being with Roger.

On Thursday, I realized it was only five days before Labor Day when my parents were coming to take me home. I'd just about given up hope that Roger would ever turn up. I decided to stop mooning about it. I'd had crushes before, and I'd gotten over them. I had a terrible crush once on Doris Berringer and spent a lot of money on a telegram I sent to the boat when her parents took her to Europe. It said, "Bon Voyage – Love, Alan." She never even thanked me for it or mentioned it for that matter. So that ended that. Then I had a crush on Ronnie Markson, and she said she had a crush on me. We hugged and hugged, but I was careful not to push my lower body against hers. She wanted to kiss, but I was afraid I'd have an orgasm so I wouldn't kiss her. She got mad, but I couldn't very well explain why, so she stopped seeing me. Then there was Mr. Gould, my English teacher, who wore tweed sports jackets and clenched a pipe in his teeth that he couldn't smoke in class. He was very handsome, and I really wanted to be like him. But he wrote an operetta that was done at school and he didn't give me a role, so that made me stop liking him. And now there was Roger, and that was going nowhere.

I decided to take my mind off it and busy myself with work. The back of the store was more cluttered than ever. Gift boxes were scattered on every surface including the two-burner stove and Nana's cot. There were several shelves above the bed that I cleared off and dusted. I spent hours arranging the boxes that I'd gathered from all over the store. The big ones were on the bottom of the shelves and the others were on top of them in graduated sizes. I had to stand on the bed in my stocking feet to reach the top shelf. When I was done, I sat on the bed and put my shoes back on. I heard Nana through the curtain.

"I could mail it for you," she said, "but there'll be a charge."

"No," a female customer replied, "I'll do it myself if you just give me a box to put it in."

"Just a minute," I heard Nana say, and she came charging through the curtain. She saw the boxes I had stacked neatly on the shelves and she climbed up on the bed with her shoes on. She was like a little gnome as she stretched her arms as far as she could to pull out one of the boxes on the bottom of the pile.

"Wait a minute, Nana," I said getting up to help her. "I'll get it for you."

"No, you don't know the one I want."

"Nana, wait. I just straightened everything out." I began to tug at her to keep her from pulling down all the boxes. She pushed my arm away and grabbed one of them, managing to let loose an avalanche of boxes that spilled to the floor. I was suddenly furious and slapped her face. She looked at me as if she'd never seen me before. Almost in slow motion, she put her hand up to her cheek.

"Vhy did you do that to me?"

She began to cry. I ran out the back door, shaking with anger and frustration. There were a couple of folding chairs somebody had forgotten to take inside. I went over to one and sat down. I was afraid I was going to cry. I buried my face in my hands and took deep breaths, trying to calm down.

"Alan, what's the matter?" I heard Mrs. Goodell say. She must have just come out of the back door of her shop.

I quickly put my hands down. "Oh nothing."

"Don't tell me nothing. Something must be wrong." She sat on the chair next to me. "Now, come on, tell me. What is it? I'm your friend."

"Oh, Mrs. G., there's no point in talking about it. It's always my grandmother. She's horrible. She's driving me crazy."

"I know, she's not easy for any of us to take. You just have to put up with her. We all do."

"Why should we?" I asked. "She never does anything nice for anybody. No one likes her. You know my mother. She can't stand her, and she likes everybody."

"Did you ever talk to your mother about her?" she asked.

"No, she never mentions her, and if I complain about my grandmother, she just says, 'she's your father's mother' and that's the end of the discussion."

Mrs. Goodell settled back in her chair. "I've had a store next to hers for years and I'm afraid she's never been any different. But I'm going to tell you something that may help you. At least it may make you understand her better. Your mother told it to me, but I guess she didn't want you to know, so we'll just keep this a secret between us."

"Of course."

"Your grandmother had two daughters in addition to your father and your uncle."

"Oh, I know. My Aunt Ethel and my Aunt Miriam. I've seen pictures of them, but they both died before I was born."

"Yes," Mrs. Goodell said. "Anyway, your grandmother brought up your father and your uncle, but she adored her two girls. She even went to work in your grandfather's photography studio just to make extra money to buy them expensive clothes. She did everything for them, she loved them so. At the end of the World War there was a terrible influenza epidemic. Millions of people died. There were no vaccines and no way of treating it. Both your aunts got sick. You couldn't get a nurse at that time, they were so busy, so your grandmother stayed with the girls around the clock. She made your father cut his classes at Harvard to help out, but as you know, they both succumbed to the disease."

"I never knew how they died."

"Your mother told me that your grandmother had a nervous breakdown afterward. That it was as if she had lived for the girls and she felt her life was over."

"But that's so many years ago." I was confused.

"There's a little bit more. And this part you mustn't let on that you know. Your father went back to college and had to take a very important exam. He hadn't had the time to study and so he didn't know some of the answers. He copied someone else's paper. The teacher caught him cheating and he was expelled. He had wanted to be an academic, but he was forced to be a photographer like your grandfather. He never made much of a success of it."

"I guess watching his sisters die was what made him so afraid of germs. But if my mother knows all that, why isn't she more sympathetic to my grandmother?"

"All right," Mrs. Goodell said, "I'll tell you one more secret you mustn't let on that you know. When your father brought your mother to meet your grandparents, your grandmother saw a big, healthy girl from the west who'd grown up on a farm, rode horses, and milked cows. Your mother told me that instead of welcoming her, your grandmother looked her up and down and said, 'Why are you alive when my daughters are dead?'"

"That's so ugly. Why would my mother marry my father after that?"

"She loved him. It's as simple as that. But the two women could never get along afterward."

"Boy, it's hard for me to believe Nana ever loved anyone."

"You'd be surprised. Everyone has love in them for someone or something." I thought in a way Mrs. Goodell was talking about herself. She stood up. "I have to go, but I hope our talk has helped. It won't change anything, but maybe it will make you feel better." She reached down and kissed me on the cheek.

"Thank you."

I watched her walk to her car in the parking lot. I sat for a long time thinking about what Mrs. Goodell had told me. I did understand more about what had made my grandmother the way she was. But did I feel differently about her? Why should I? She had never paid any attention to anything I did to make the shop look better. She never once commented on my having a big sale. It was almost like she was competing against me and trying to top me all the time. It made no sense. I was working for her, not myself. And she was my grandmother. There wasn't a moment when she showed any affection or even the slightest interest in me. But now I knew that she had her own problems. I guess she was never able to solve them.

I went back into the store. Nana had made herself some tea and was just picking up a cup. I somehow managed to get out the words, "I'm sorry, Nana." She just looked at me in her usual unseeing way and walked into the front of the shop.

At the end of the day, when I was carrying in the baskets from the sidewalk, Roger drove up and parked his car in front of the store. As he got out, I walked over to him and said, "Hi."

He seemed rather formal and said that he was on his way to a dinner and couldn't stay more than a minute. "It occurred to me," he said, "that next weekend is Labor Day, and I always wanted to do a bicycle trip in Martha's Vineyard. Maybe you'd want to go along."

He seemed so distant and impersonal that I hesitated. I should have been overjoyed, but I felt as if I were a kid being asked by a friend of my father's to go on a camping trip. After all my anticipation of seeing him again, our meeting was so disappointing and anti-climactic. But I said, "Sure. I would like to very much."

Roger had to work on Saturday, so we planned to leave Sunday, stay overnight and return on Monday.

"Do you think your grandmother will mind?" he asked.

"I don't care what she does," I said, still smarting from the incident with the boxes.

"Well, we better ask her anyway," he said and walked into the shop as I trailed behind.

Roger was incredibly charming to the old woman who wasn't used to any kind of attention. He told her many of his friends thought her store was the best on the Byway. He buttered her up so much that when he asked her permission to take me on a bicycle trip, she said yes. Besides, no one had ever asked her permission about anything before. Roger told me to come to his house Sunday morning at eight since he was closer to Woods Hole where we'd get the ferry.

As soon as he left, Nana seemed to come to her senses. "Who vas that?" she asked as soon as the door closed.

"Roger Alton," I answered. "I just introduced you."

"How'd you meet him?" her eyes narrowed craftily.

"Through some friends," I lied.

"Who?"

"What's the difference? You seemed to like him."

"He vas all right, but you're not going on any trip with him."

We argued all through dinner at the Elm Tree. Finally, I'd had it. "Nana, I've worked all summer and I've never had any fun. I've always wanted to see Martha's Vineyard and I'm going to."

"But who is he?" she repeated.

"He works at that big landscaping place near the train station. He knows I don't have any friends here, so I guess he's being nice to me. I haven't asked you for anything else and it's only going to cost a couple of dollars, just enough for the meals and a cheap room. Can't you give me this one thing?"

I knew it wasn't easy for her since I'd slapped her only a few hours before. But finally, she said, "Leave me alone."

I knew it would be all right.

Chapter 15

I woke up and reached for my watch, but the radium dial was too dim so I couldn't see the time. I put the light on and groaned. It was only four o'clock. I still had three hours before I could get up. I lay awake thinking about the day to come. What would I talk about with Roger? I was going to spend two days with someone who was twice my age that I didn't know well. If only I'd had more of an education, or I'd paid more attention to current events. Then I thought, what would I wear? I didn't have anything nice, just an old pair of slacks and some shirts. Even my good sweater had a hole in it.

Also, I probably didn't have enough money. I'd somehow managed to get ten dollars from Nana, but would that be enough for two days? What if I ran out? Could I borrow from somebody I didn't even know? Why did Roger ask me in the first place? He hadn't seemed very friendly when he came by the shop. Why did I tell him that I didn't have any friends? That must have been the reason he asked me to go with him. He felt sorry for me. He must have thought I was just a lonely, pathetic kid who ought to be given an outing.

I turned out the light and tried to get comfortable. I rolled over on my left side and put the pillow on top of my head. It was cool, so I pulled up the thin blanket to just below my nose. I tried not to think about anything, but the talk I had with Nana, after I had gotten the money out of her, kept coming back.

She had changed her mind and said I couldn't go and threatened to call my parents if I did. They weren't supposed to come from Brookline to pick me up until after Monday. What if they came earlier? They'd be sure to make a fuss. And then, if Roger met them, he'd know that I was Jewish. He must have wondered about Nana, anyway. Would he want to be friends with me if he knew I was Jewish?

I must have slept for a while because I suddenly woke up in a panic. I grabbed my watch, terrified that I'd overslept. But it was just six-thirty. I sighed with relief and decided to get out of bed. It was too early, but at least I'd be out of the house and could avoid seeing Nana again.

The town was at its quietest since it was Sunday. There were no trucks on the highway, and it was too early for the churchgoers. I rode around aimlessly waiting until it was time to pick up Roger at his house. I had folded a paper bag neatly and put it in the basket of my bicycle with a clean shirt, underwear and a toothbrush. I was wearing my sweater since the sun had not yet warmed the salt air that comes from the sea. The trees were heavy with leaves and the grass was a rich green. In only a few weeks, everything would start to shrivel up with the early frost, but it still looked like the height of summer now.

At five minutes to eight, I turned onto Pin Oak Way. I hadn't wanted to arrive early and appear too eager. Roger was waiting in front of a newly built, two story clapboard Colonial with plantings of bushes and hollyhocks. He was rather cool greeting me and said we'd better get going or we'd miss the nine o'clock ferry. I rode in front of him for the four miles to Woods Hole. Our bikes were too far apart for us to talk, so I pedaled as fast as I could to show Roger that I wouldn't be a burden on the trip. The sun had still not appeared, and I was afraid it was going to be a gray day.

When we reached the ferry, there was a sign that said: "Martha's Vineyard – $1.30 Round Trip – Bikes Free." I insisted on paying my way and for the first time since I'd picked him up, Roger smiled. He had seemed so preoccupied that I had begun to wish I hadn't come, but his wonderful smile made me feel differently. We dragged our bikes onboard and got a good place at the railing on the upper deck so we could watch the approach to the Vineyard. The trip took less than an hour and the island was in sight the whole way. The sun came out and reflected on the water so we both had to reach for our sunglasses to cut the glare. Hidden behind them, we both seemed more able to talk to each other. By the time we could make out the houses at Oak Bluffs, we were talking like we had been that day at the beach, and I felt so much better.

The docking of the ferry was pandemonium—tourists rushing to get off, the line of cars moving too slowly, hotel porters holding signs looking for guests, and people getting onboard for the next leg of the journey to Nantucket. We managed to push our way through to where the bikes were stored and got off as quickly as we could. It seemed almost like we were refugees leaving one of the bombed cities that I saw in the newsreels at the movies.

Once we were on the road, past the saltwater taffy stands, the crowd thinned out. We found the sign pointing to Vineyard Haven. As we biked through Oak Bluffs, we passed Victorian houses with fretwork fronts that looked like gingerbread cutouts. Roger remarked at how ugly they were, and I agreed.

Vineyard Haven was different—a beautiful church with a white spire and Colonial houses impeccably kept behind picket-fenced, old-fashioned gardens. We were in the Martha's Vineyard that I had always dreamed of visiting. I wanted to wander through the town, but Roger said we had a lot of ground to cover if we were going to get around the island in one day.

The sun was out fully by now and it was very hot. The landscape was flat and uninteresting and didn't change as we rode along. I saw a sign for Lambert's Cove that pointed away from our route on the main road. I asked Roger if we could go see it. I had a vision of a hidden place by the sea where we could stop for a swim. He agreed and we took a detour for seven miles to a stretch of rough sand and several plain houses.

"I'm sorry," I said, "but the name sounded so great."

"Don't be silly. It doesn't matter. We're just exploring."

I was grateful that he didn't blame me. We talked very little as we rode, concentrating on changing the gears on our bikes as we pumped up the gentle hills. After a few hours, we arrived at a huge bluff surrounded on three sides by the sea. A sign told us we were in Gay Head. We left our bikes leaning against a tree and climbed down a path through multi-colored clay cliffs. I walked in front of Roger, and as I came onto the beach, I saw a woman with a baby lying on a towel. The straps were down on her bathing suit. For an instant, I saw her breasts, but she quickly covered them. I walked beyond her to a hidden place farther down the beach. Roger followed me and we both went in back of separate rocks to put on our bathing suits.

The ocean was rough, and more rocks were in the water so we couldn't swim. We splashed about, relieved to cool our bodies still hot from the sun and the strenuous ride. When we had dried off, we went behind the rocks again to dress. As we started to climb up past the orange and red cliffs, I said, "Boy am I hungry."

"I forgot to tell you that the closest restaurant is ten miles away."

"Oh," I groaned, "I don't think I can make it."

Roger laughed. "Don't worry."

There was a weather-beaten farmhouse near where we had put our bikes. He left me and went up on the porch and knocked on the door. A gray-haired, middle-aged woman in a faded housedress came out, and I could hear him talking to her, but I couldn't make out the words. When he returned, he was laughing.

"I told her we weren't beggars and that we'd pay for the food, so she's going to make us sandwiches."

"Hooray!"

The woman brought us thickly sliced ham on homemade bread and two glasses of ice-cold milk. I tried to pay my share, but Roger wouldn't let me. We sat in the shade of a huge maple tree and savored each bite as if it were the most superb gourmet food. When we finished, Roger took a candy bar out of his small duffle bag and broke it in half.

"Dessert?" he asked and handed me a piece. We both lay on the grass munching the chocolate, totally content.

The ride that afternoon was a nightmare. It was mostly through scrub pines and flat, uninteresting land with only an occasional house. We never found one store where we could get a cold drink. Neither of us was used to bicycling so much, and our legs ached. We stood up on our pedals as we rode as often as we could to take the strain off our bottoms.

With each passing mile, I grew more uncomfortable. There was no longer any fun between us, and we didn't speak at all. I wanted, more than anything, to get off my bicycle and lie down somewhere, but the road kept going on and on.

As it was getting dark, we came to Edgartown which seemed like we'd reached civilization after spending days in the desert. Even more beautiful than Vineyard Haven, it was still somehow unwelcoming. The shops were closed and there were very few people in the streets. It was like a museum shut down for the night. We rode around the deserted town looking for a place to stay. We finally found a white clapboard house badly in need of paint with a sign that said "Rooms." The landlady showed us a room up one flight of stairs with twin beds. She said it was the last one she had because of the holiday. It was barely clean, and the wooden furniture was painted a bilious green. We were afraid to look further so we each paid a dollar, washed quickly, and set off to find supper.

We wandered down to the harbor. A low, flat building that looked like a diner was harshly lit. Through the window, we could see a counter and several tables. A sign outside that read "Lobsters" encouraged us, so we went in. We were given a table that a bored waitress washed off with a dirty, wet cloth. I hardly said a word. The place was so depressing and the thought of going back to that ugly room made me wish I'd never come. Even Roger seemed ordinary in this shoddy setting.

The lobster, however, was excellent. My mother had always planned for me to have a rich life that she dreamed of, so she had taught me how to use a finger bowl and eat lobster properly. As a result, I felt secure, in front of Roger, digging the meat out of the claws and sucking the juice from each of the legs. He made a few attempts at conversation, praising the lobster, saying there must be sherry in the butter sauce. He gave up after a while and we ate in silence. He insisted on paying the check since he'd drunk some wine. He said it wouldn't be fair to split it in half. I was too tired to argue.

When we got back to the room, Roger suggested that I take my bath first. The bathroom was down the hall and I found a tub with a makeshift shower attachment. I watched the water, brown from the dust of the road, run down my chest and into the drain. The skimpy shower curtain stuck to my body. It was difficult soaping myself with one hand while holding the curtain out of the way with the other. Then I dried off, put on clean underwear, went back to the room, and got into bed.

There was a Martha's Vineyard brochure on the nightstand, and I thumbed through it, checking out the places we'd been while Roger took his bath. It was hot and stuffy. We had made it even worse by closing the window, because there were no screens to keep out the mosquitoes. When Roger returned, he immediately got into his bed. After only a few minutes, we decided it was better getting bitten than dying from the heat, so Roger got out of bed in his shorts and opened the window. He raised the paper shade so we might get even a slight breeze. Just outside was the electrified "Rooms" sign, so when Roger turned out the light, the room stayed almost as bright as it had been before.

"I just heard a mosquito," I said.

"Don't think about it. Goodnight."

"Goodnight."

I lay awake for what seemed like hours. Every once in a while, I'd turn to a different position trying not to make any noise so I wouldn't wake Roger. There wasn't a breath of air coming through the window and not a sound came from the street below. I thought the night would never end.

"What's the matter? Can't you sleep?" I heard him say. He was turned away from me, so I had thought he was asleep.

"I don't know, I just don't feel sleepy." There was a long silence.

"Do you want to talk?" he suddenly said.

"Sure," I replied.

"What do you want to talk about?"

"I don't know. Anything."

"Well, why don't you tell me about your friends," he suggested.

"You mean at home or in Falmouth?"

"Whatever you want."

I was relieved not to have to try to sleep any longer, so I talked about Brookline. I told him about Irving Leavitt and how we crashed parties together. I also spoke about my "kind of" girlfriend, Nancy Williams, who was at camp in Silver Beach. I confessed that she wasn't very pretty.

"Actually," I said, "she's short and stocky, and it's hard for me to feel romantic about her. I did take a pretty girl, Ronnie Markson, to the Junior Prom. She's very rich and I felt uncomfortable, as if I wasn't good enough for her, so I didn't see her again."

"What about your friends in Falmouth?"

"Well, they're just the people in the shops. Connie, I guess was my best friend, but since she met Lester, I never see her. I like Liz Sherman okay, but she's a bit of a phony. Then there's Mrs. Goodell and Jim. They're nice, but they're always fighting." I stopped. I took a deep breath. I looked over at Roger's profile. "Do you know Dave Garland who has the antique store?" I asked, trying to make it as inconsequential as possible. But I somehow knew I was opening a can of worms.

"Yes," Roger replied.

There was something funny about the way he said it. There was some mystery that I felt he knew. So, to provoke him to say more, I said, "I like him." There was a long silence and I was afraid I'd said something that had ended the conversation.

Finally, Roger said, "Do you wish he was here with you now instead of me?"

"Of course not." I felt there was something odd in what he'd asked me. I didn't say anything more for a moment, but I couldn't leave it alone. "Why would I?"

"You know."

I felt I was opening a door to a mysterious passageway, but I couldn't resist it. "No, I don't know. What do you mean?"

"You know perfectly well."

"But I don't." Then I added, "I like him, but he makes me uncomfortable."

"I'm sure he does," Roger replied.

There was something knowing in the way he said it that made me want to contradict him, but instead I said, "There's something funny about him." I waited for him to respond to that, but he didn't. There was another silence and I felt my chest getting tight. "He wants me to go nude swimming with him all the time." I was lying. He'd only asked me once, but I had to make it more important so I could get Roger to say something that he seemed to be hiding.

"I'll bet he does," Roger said. "Have you ever gone?"

"Of course not. Why would I?"

"Why not? Were you afraid?"

"No, I thought it sounded silly for two men to go swimming nude."

"Didn't you think anything about it?" Roger asked

I felt as if I were being forced into a corner. "What do you mean?"

"Didn't you wonder why he wanted you to go with him?"

"No," I almost shouted.

"I'll bet you did," Roger said. "I'll bet you wanted to go."

I felt frightened. There was something bubbling up in me that I wasn't sure I wanted to let out. Then I did. I said, "If I'd wanted to, I would have." I lay expectantly in my bed not moving a muscle. There was a long silence again.

"Did he ever try to kiss you?"

As soon as I heard the word "kiss" I thought my heart had stopped. I didn't want Roger to know what I was feeling so I forced myself to answer in as flat a voice as possible. "Of course not, why would he?"

I stole a look at Roger who was staring at the ceiling. "You know about him, don't you?"

Suddenly I realized for the first time that there was something I wanted to know, but I'd been avoiding it. "What do you mean?" I asked.

"That he likes boys."

"No, I didn't know that." But I wasn't telling the whole truth.

"Do you think that's so awful?"

I could barely breathe, but I managed to say, "No, of course not."

"I like boys too," he said.

I was looking away from him. I felt cold and I was afraid I was going to cry. "Roger," I said, "I'm freezing."

For a moment there wasn't a sound and then he said, "Do you want to come into my bed?"

I began to shake. "Please, you come over here," I could barely say the words.

"No," he said sternly, "you have to come to me."

"I can't. I'm shaking."

"Then don't," he said, but there was nothing mean in the way he said it.

I lay helplessly on my bed, trembling as if I were having a fit. I was desperate to be warm again. I managed to get out of my bed and cross the few feet to his. I got in beside him and he opened his arms to me. I buried my face in his neck. He pulled my head back and kissed me on the lips. I was stunned for a moment. I'd always thought you needed lipstick to kiss on the lips and that's why women wore it. I realized I had an erection and I kissed him back. Almost immediately I had an orgasm. I lay panting in Roger's arms.

"I'm so sorry," I said. "I just couldn't help it."

"Don't be silly," he said. "Just relax."

We lay entwined. When I could breathe normally again, I got up and took off my wet underwear. Roger reached out to me and I got back into his bed. We kissed again, and though we hardly moved against each other, we had several orgasms, and I fell asleep in his arms.

Chapter 16

When I awoke the next morning, it took me a minute to remember where I was. Then the whole experience with Roger came back to me. I was in my own bed so I must have left Roger at some time during the night. I shut my eyes. I felt so depressed and disgusted. If only it hadn't happened. All I could think of was the time I was caught stealing in the Five and Ten when I was a kid. The same sick feeling was in the pit of my stomach and the same dread that my whole life was ruined. I forced myself to look over at Roger's bed. There was no movement from under the tangle of sheet and blanket that covered the mound of a sleeping body.

I got up as quietly as I could and showered. I felt nauseous as I scrubbed away at the remains of our lovemaking. I kept going over and over the experience in my mind. How could I have done it? How could I have let Roger take advantage of me? Yes, that was it. He had taken advantage of me. But no, I had gone to his bed. But I didn't know what would happen. Well, I did know something would, though I wasn't exactly sure what it would be. But still it was Roger's fault. He was old enough to know what was going on. I didn't, but whatever it was, I had wanted it. Back and forth I went, trying to find some way out for myself, but I couldn't.

Finally, after rubbing my body harshly with the towel, as if I were erasing what had happened, I went back to the room. He was still asleep, so I dressed quietly. As I was putting my few things in the paper bag, I could feel him looking at me.

"Good morning," Roger said.

I looked over at him. His hair was sticking up where he had slept on it and I could see it was thinning. His ears seemed like two handles on a vase and there was a silly smirk on his face. How could I ever have thought that he was handsome? He looked ugly. I knew I had to stay with him until we got back to Falmouth. I looked at him coldly and said, "I'll wait for you out on the street." I turned and left the room.

We ate breakfast in silence. He had taken his cue from me and only spoke when he asked me to pass him the cream and sugar. The tone of his voice was impersonal, and I was careful to keep any warmth out of my voice. We split the check, got on our bikes and headed to Oak Bluffs to get the ferry back to Woods Hole. The day was cloudy and only added to my depression. After an hour, the sun did come out, but it didn't help. I rode ahead of Roger and only looked back to see if he was still following me. We rode for miles along a deserted beach that lined the north side of the island. I heard Roger calling my name, so I stopped.

"What's the hurry?" he said as he pulled up beside me. "We're almost there and we've got two hours before the ferry leaves." I didn't answer him. "Why don't we get some sun on the beach?"

"I want to go home."

"I know you do, but I don't want to sit around in Oak Bluffs for hours." He waited for me to say something, When I didn't, he said, "I'm going to swim. You can do what you want."

There was no malice in the way that he said it. Actually, he looked at me warmly and then took his bike over to a spot on the sand and laid it down. He stripped down to his shorts and went in the water. I thought for a minute about going in by myself, but I didn't want to be anywhere near him. I took my bike a distance away from his and sat dejectedly looking at the sea. I didn't take off any of my clothes, and the heat made me even more miserable.

Roger came out of the water, dried himself, and then spread his towel neatly on the sand. When he sat down, he looked over at me. I was letting sand pour idly through my fingers.

"Come on," he said, and his voice had nothing but kindness in it. "It's not that bad."

I was afraid I was going to cry. I forced myself to look at him. His body was still wet from the sea and his shoulder bones protruded from his thin frame. He smiled at me with that extraordinary smile I still hadn't gotten used to. I ran over to him and threw my arms around his neck.

"I love you," I said.

Chapter 17

The sky clouded over. The ferry was being tossed about by the rough sea. I stood as close as I could to Roger, being careful not to touch him in a way that might be noticed. The wind blew my hair and my eyes began to tear, but I wasn't cold. I had a secret and it was creating a warm place in my chest. Everything was decided. I had what I had been longing for all   only a friend, but someone to love. I didn't even question whether I was loved back. I just felt that the future was secure. Now I would have someone to guide me and help me learn all the right things. I looked toward the land that we were approaching and thought about how it would be. I would graduate in June and then go to drama school in New York. Roger would live there with me. I couldn't say it out loud now for fear someone would hear me, but I would tell Roger as soon as we were alone.

I looked at him now as if for the first time. How handsome he was. With his thin, straight nose and his prominent cheekbones, he looked like the pictures of the Pilgrims in my American history book. He had told me that his ancestors came over on the Mayflower, and I could picture him in the black hat with the buckle and the white ruff. Actually, I was thinking of a costume from my grammar school Thanksgiving play made up of clothes our mothers had lent, but I was sure that's the way Roger would have looked.

"I'm going to get us some coffee," Roger said.

I saw him walk, as steadily as he could, to the stairs that led below. The boat was pitching, and I had to hold onto the railing. I watched Woods Hole come closer and closer until Roger got back. I took the cardboard cup from him as if he were giving me a precious gift and I sipped the bitter coffee. We were almost ready to dock. I looked casually at the crowds ready to board. Suddenly I froze.

"It's my parents," I gasped. "What'll we do?"

"Where?"

"Right there on the dock. See that woman in the flowered dress and the man with the glasses next to her? They look furious."

"Don't worry," he said, "I'll take care of it."

"My God, they'll know—"

Roger touched my arm. "There's nothing for them to know. We've just been on a bicycle trip."

At that moment my mother caught sight of me. I smiled and waved to her. She looked grim but I pretended not to notice it. I pointed down below where I would meet them. I turned and walked to the stairs and Roger followed me.

When we were out of my mother's sight, he said, "Just leave it to me."

"I'm so sorry. they're going to be just awful."

"No, they're not," he reassured me, and he was right. He knew, better than I did, what he was capable of doing. The landing was accomplished quickly since the ferry was so small. Roger and I walked over to my parents, who didn't kiss me or say hello.

"This is the third ferry we've met," my mother said glaring at me. "You worried me half to death. I'll never forgive you for this."

"Please, Mother," I said, "everything's okay. This is Roger Alton. These are my parents, Roger."

"I would have recognized you immediately, Mrs. Schein," Roger said, "Alan looks so like you. And I'm terribly sorry. I should have called you and Mr. Schein instead of Alan's grandmother for your approval to take him to the Vineyard. But I thought it would be perfectly all right."

My father seemed embarrassed at my mother's rudeness. "You understand we just didn't know you," he said, "so we got worried about Alan being away overnight."

"I would have felt the same way," Roger said. "It's just that we've been spending a lot of time recently talking about Alan's future. He's been asking me about college, and I've been trying to convince him to go. I thought the trip would be good for him and we could really talk it through."

"Oh, that's very nice of you," my father said. "We certainly agree with that. Where did you go to college, Mr. Alton?"

"Mass State."

"In Amherst," my father said. "That's a very good school."

"It was perfect for me because I wanted to be a landscape architect, but I don't think it's quite the place for Alan. We've been running through a list of other colleges. By the way, please call me Roger."

"You do understand," my mother suddenly said, "that we worried about Alan being with a stranger."

"Of course, I would have worried too if it were my son."

My parents found themselves apologizing to Roger for having doubted him. He was suddenly in the position of forgiving *them*, and I just stood by as if I were watching a tennis match.

Now that everything was resolved, it was decided that we couldn't get my bicycle in Dad's car, so I would ride back to Falmouth with Roger.

"Don't take too long," my mother said, "we should leave right after supper, and you have to pack."

"What do you mean?" It was the first time I'd spoken since I'd introduced Roger to them.

"You're going back to Brookline with us. Nana has to have some X-rays tomorrow, so we have to go back tonight."

"But why?" I asked trying not to show my panic in my voice. "I don't have to be back in school until next Monday–"

"Well, there's no point in your staying another week. Nobody will come into the shop after Labor Day."

"Please," I begged them, "can't I just stay until Daddy brings Nana back? I may do a little business and I can say goodbye to my friends." I was embarrassed to act like a little boy in front of Roger, but I had to find a way to stay.

"We'll talk about it back at the shop," my father said.

"I hope you can come to the shop and have coffee with us," my mother said to Roger.

"I'd like to very much, but I'm afraid I have a dinner date."

"If you ever get to Boston," Dad said, "you must come over and have dinner with us. Mrs. Schein is a very good cook."

"I'm sure she is, and I'd like to very much," he said.

Roger and my parents said their goodbyes with smiles all around and promised to meet soon. Then we hopped on our bikes and set off for Falmouth.

At first there were a lot of cars coming off the ferry, then it quieted down and there was just the two of us. The sky above was still light but the road in front was as dark as if night had come. My father's car passed by. Mother waved gaily from her window and we both waved back. It seemed like all was forgiven. Roger had saved the day.

I signaled to him that I wanted to stop. We found a grassy bank where we could pull off the road. As soon as we were together, he said, "We mustn't stay more than a minute, or they'll wonder why we're so late."

"I know, but what'll we do if they force me to go back with them?"

"Don't worry. I'm sure they'll let you stay a couple of more days."

"You don't know them," I held the side of my head with one hand. "I just can't leave you until we have a chance to talk about everything."

"If they let you stay, we'll do it tonight," he said.

"But you said you had to go out for dinner—"

He smiled. "Don't be silly."

Roger turned off when we came to Pin Oak Way. We'd arranged for me to come to his house if my parents didn't force me to leave. I hurried to the store. I didn't want to waste any more time before confronting my parents. I kept going over and over in my mind the moment on the beach when I realized I loved Roger. I felt no shame about it now. It seemed so natural, as if it had been planned from the very first time that I saw him, laughing with the two women. It seemed to me that I loved him even then. As if for years, I had been guided to this time and place. I felt like a runner who had been encouraged by pats on the back from the spectators along the track. I hadn't even known about love between two men – there were no books about it – but somehow, I sensed it from the time I hid the picture of the nude boy on the wall of my bedroom. I guess it had always been a part of me.

My parents were not a problem. Without any argument at all, they said I could stay the week. Roger had won them over completely and they wanted to know all about him. They were flattered that he had taken such an interest in me. They encouraged me to invite him up to Brookline. We ate the sandwiches Mother had brought and had some soup she heated on the hot plate. I couldn't wait to see them go, but I tried to act as natural as possible.

I even managed to say, "Do you have to go so soon?" as they started to leave.

Mother grabbed me and kissed me wetly. "Oh, I love you so much."

As soon as they left, I sped over to Roger's house. I recognized the man who opened the door. I had seen him working at the Five and Ten. He told me that Roger's room was at the top of the stairs on the left. I knew he rented a furnished room, but I was startled at how small it was. When he let me in, we barely had room to stand in a space between the double bed and a small desk.

Roger closed the door and held me for a minute. "I knew you'd be here," he said as he guided me a few steps to a chair. I sat with my knees touching the bed while Roger stretched out. "Don't talk too loudly," he whispered, "the Smith's room is right across the hall."

I told him how glad I was not to have to go back with my parents. "I don't know what I would have done if I hadn't been able to see you."

"You would have seen me," he replied. "I would have come up to Boston before you knew it."

"What are we going to do?" I said trying not to sound as desperate as I felt.

"Well, right now, we're not going to do anything. We're going to listen to some music and not talk for a while. Do you like classical music?"

"My father plays it on the radio, usually on Sundays. It's very heavy music and it always depresses me. There are two pieces I do like: the '1812 Overture' and Enesco's 'Romanian Dances.' I guess I just don't understand that kind of music," I said hoping he wouldn't be annoyed with me.

"Well, let's just listen together and see if I can't help you." He got up and put a record on a small player attached to a radio. Then he lay down on the bed again.

"Can I lie there beside you?" I asked.

"Yes," he said, "but no distractions."

I lay beside him as the record began. I was swept up immediately in the music. "That's the beginning of the Orson Welles radio show," I said, excited that I had recognized it.

"It's the Tchaikovsky 'Piano Concerto,'" Roger corrected me. "Just listen." He turned out the lights and lit a cigarette. He gave me a puff. I didn't inhale but I just blew the smoke out slowly, copying him. When the theme I had recognized from the radio show was finished, I asked him to play it again.

"You have to hear the whole work," he said, "not just an excerpt or you'll grow tired of it."

I wanted to talk about our life together and make some plans for the future, but he quieted me down.

"There's plenty of time for that," he said. I kissed him but that was all he would let me do. "We didn't get much sleep last night, so we'd better be sensible."

I was content just to be next to him and savor the smell of the smoke mingling with the Old Spice aftershave. When the concerto finished, he put on another record.

"This is Schubert's 'The Trout,'" he said. "Now just forget that it's classical music and try to imagine a fish jumping and splashing in a brook, alive and free. If you listen carefully, you'll hear it swimming through the water. You may even know when the fisherman catches it."

I concentrated really hard and I was sure I was getting it right.

Roger took my hand. "Don't make such an effort," he said, "it takes a little time." He stopped the record in the middle. "You've got to go home and I'm exhausted."

"Please let me stay," I begged, but he wouldn't be persuaded.

"I've got to be at work early in the morning."

I remembered that I had been given two passes for the Cape Playhouse for the next evening. All the shops got them for putting posters in the windows. I told Roger about it and asked him if he'd go with me.

"Only if you leave right now," he said jokingly.

"I will, I will."

We kissed goodbye—a long kiss—and I ran down the stairs and out of the house to my bike. Only when I got halfway to the rooming house did I remember that nothing had been decided about our future.

Chapter 18

The next day seemed interminable. Only a few people came into the shop, and I didn't know what to do with myself. I stood and stared out the front window hoping that Roger would come by. Then I went in the back and tried to read but couldn't. I took a chair out the side door to the parking lot to get a little more of a tan, but I couldn't sit still.

I went next door to see Mrs. Goodell. We'd become even more friendly, and I often talked to her. I stayed near her back door where I could hear anyone going into the shop and called out to her. She came out, her mouth full of pins and a skirt over her arm.

"Where've you been," she mumbled. "Jim was going to rent a sailboat and take you fishing, but he couldn't find you."

I told her as much as I could about the weekend with Roger. She watched me closely as I kept extolling Roger's qualities. When I'd finished, she said, "Are you going to see him again?"

"Of course," I replied. "We're going to the Cape Playhouse tonight."

"Does he have a girlfriend?" Mrs. Goodell asked.

"I guess so," I said thrown completely off guard.

"Well just be careful. I don't think it's good for you to be alone too much with a man so much older. Why don't you introduce him to Liz? It sounds like they might get along."

"Sure," I said, but I wished I'd kept my mouth shut. Mrs. Goodell seemed to sense the change in my mood.

"He hasn't done anything to you, has he?" she asked.

"Of course not. He's not like that."

"Well, I wouldn't see too much of him, that's all. Even if there's nothing wrong with him, you never can tell what can happen."

"I'm leaving the day after tomorrow, Mrs. G. I probably won't see him again."

"It's better you're with someone your own age," she said, and closed the subject.

Roger picked me up at six. I'd gone all the way back to the rooming house to put on my best jacket and a tie. He told me how nice I looked. We went to a restaurant in Yarmouth Port where he had worked ten years before. It had very low ceilings with old beams. Each table had a candle burning in a hurricane lamp. The people at the other tables were all either fifty or sixty. I felt very awkward and self-conscious. Mrs. Goodell had disturbed me so much that I couldn't help looking at Roger differently. Why had Mrs. G. wondered about him? Did he seem strange? I suddenly felt that everyone was looking at us. Did they know? He talked about his day at the nursery and a new client who was putting in huge trees that were costing a fortune. I worried that he was talking too loudly. And was his voice a little too high?

At the theater, we sat in the back with the rest of the people who'd gotten in free. The play was *Her Cardboard Lover* and the star was Tallulah Bankhead. She had a deep, throaty voice and managed to make everything she said have a sexy double meaning. Roger kept roaring with laughter. I looked around to see if people were staring at us. Was his laugh higher than it should be? I couldn't get my mind off what Mrs. Goodell had implied. I could barely follow the plot and I longed to get away and be alone with him. Maybe then I could lose this awful feeling of something being wrong.

Once we were in the car and driving back to Falmouth, all of my doubts disappeared. Roger smoked and concentrated on the road ahead. We both listened to the radio. "Indian Summer," that was so popular then, was playing and I felt as if I were in a movie with the perfect background music. There was a chill in the air, but I had gotten Roger to put the top down. I sat close to him. I was no longer alone, and it didn't matter what people said or thought.

"Would you like to sleep overnight with me?" he asked.

I couldn't believe my good fortune. "But what about your landlord?"

"He won't see you leaving in the morning, and if he does, I'll say it was too late for you to go home."

When we were in bed, he reached over and pulled up the window shade so we could see the moon. We lay in each other's arms and kissed. After a moment, I pulled away from our embrace and started to touch my lips to Roger's chest. I then moved down toward his stomach. I felt my head being pulled back.

"What are you doing?" Roger whispered.

"I want to kiss all of you," I said.

"No," he said sternly. "Don't!"

"Why not?"

"It isn't right." He sounded really annoyed.

"But what could be wrong about it?" I insisted.

"How many other men have you been with like this?"

"None. You know that. I've told you—only the boy at the summer camp, and that was nothing like us."

"Oh, come on, don't kid me."

"But I haven't been with anyone else," I protested. "Can't you tell?"

"You certainly seem to know a lot," he said sullenly. "Why did you want to do that?"

"It seemed so natural.,"

"Well, it isn't. Let's go to sleep."

"Please don't be angry. I just didn't know."

"Forget about it." He turned on his side away from me and wouldn't say anything more.

I lay awake. I was so frustrated and miserable. What had I done? I couldn't figure it out. I went over and over it. I thought I was being loving. What was so wrong? And then something came into my head. Something from my childhood that I had buried and not thought about for years. I forced myself to go over it. Maybe it was the key to what had upset Roger so much, so I could avoid it ever happening again.

It was when I was seven or eight. We were living in Falmouth in the little house in back of Uncle Louis and Aunt Rae's big house. I was allowed to play on their porch. It was hidden. Heavy vines crawled over three sides of it, leaving just the screen door uncovered. It was a perfect place to hide. They said I was too big for dolls now, but I found some sticks and took silver paper from cigarette packs that I rolled into balls and pushed onto the end of the sticks. They looked like little people to me, and I cradled them lovingly in my hands. I hid them over the swinging sofa on the porch. I only got to play with them when no one was around. If my parents found them, they would say they were dolls and take them away.

I was playing with my sticks one day when I suddenly heard a cry of "Alan" from the garden. It was my brother, too close for comfort. I rushed to the swinging sofa and managed to get up on it as it swayed back and forth. I shoved the figures out of sight. Again, the loud cry of "Alan." I jumped down and ran out of the porch, slamming the rickety screen door that barely closed anymore. I ran around the house into the garden.

"Where the hell were you?" Donald demanded as he paced back and forth. "It's bad enough having to mind you, but I'm not going to run all over the place trying to find you."

"I'm sorry. I was right here."

"C'mon." He walked toward the woods. He was five years older than me, so I had to really run to keep up with him.

We set off through the woods toward a pile of old broken liquor bottles that I thought had pirates' treasure buried beneath them. I'd always wanted to dig there, but I'd cut myself when I tried once. I was just waiting until I grew up enough to have something better than a sand shovel to use.

"Where are we going?" I asked.

"Ask me no questions and I'll tell you no lies," he answered me in a singsong voice.

"I want to know."

"Let's go home, and I'll lock you in the house. I don't want a crybaby with me."

"Please, please. Let me go with you."

"All right but hurry up."

There was a deer path through the woods, and we followed it. We had to watch out for the poison ivy that was everywhere. I had learned to recognize it since I got it so badly and swelled up like a balloon. I had never been in this part of the woods, and I hurried to keep up with Donald's longer strides. We went through a grove of pines. All the lower branches were without needles, I guess from the lack of sun. It was like a dead place and I felt a chill.

After about ten minutes, we came to a ramshackle lean-to. We had gradually been going higher up. It was now very rocky and heavily wooded. Only a few slanting rays of sun managed to get through to this place, so it was cold and dark.

Donald banged at an old door hanging on one hinge of the shack. Immediately it popped open and revealed a very tall man in his twenties with an ugly scar on his upper lip.

"Where the hell have you been?" he said. Then he glared at me. "What'd ya bring him for?"

Donald said sheepishly, "I had to mind him, so I had to bring him along."

"I wanted to come," I said trying to let the giant know that I wasn't a baby.

"Where's the food?" the young man asked.

I noticed for the first time that Donald was carrying a paper bag that he handed over. The man grabbed it, tore it open, and started gobbling some thick sandwiches that were badly wrapped in used wax paper. He went into the shed and Donald followed him, pushing me in as well. We sat down on the earth floor.

"This is Franklin's secret place," Donald whispered to me. "You can never tell where it is."

Franklin paid no attention to either of us as he finished wolfing down the food. I suddenly remembered that Franklin was the name my father had used one night when he was having an argument with Donald. My father had said that he didn't want Donald hanging around with Franklin Pease. That he was twice Donald's age and had been in reform school. But Donald said Franklin had promised to take him hunting. My father was furious. I remember him saying, "I won't have you spending any time with him, and that's final!"

I watched Franklin finish the last of the food. He rolled up all the paper in a ball and threw it in a corner. The shed was quite dark but there was enough light for me to see his eyes gleaming.

"Come here, little boy," he said.

I didn't say anything. I knew something awful was going to happen. I looked at Donald, but he was looking away, pretending to be unconcerned. Franklin stood up. He towered over the two of us sitting on the ground. He was wearing old blue overalls that the trainmen wore. He undid two brass buttons on his shoulders and pulled the overalls down. He then pushed his underwear down to his knees and exposed himself. He walked over to me.

"Open your mouth," he said. He grabbed a big piece of wood covered with rusty nails. "If you bite me, I'll kill you with this."

I began to cry.

"Open your mouth." He put both his hands on my head and forced my mouth open, pushing himself in as far as he could.

Tears poured out of my eyes and I thought I would choke. I couldn't breathe and my throat was hurting because he was so big. I was afraid I would throw up. I kept praying that Donald would help me, but he didn't. Franklin pushed in and out, holding my mouth open and hitting me on the head if I moved. After what seemed like hours, Franklin stopped and pulled out of my mouth. He turned to Donald who was still sitting quietly. "Take off your pants," he said.

I just stayed where I was, crying softly. I watched Franklin put Donald's tiny thing in his mouth. I closed my eyes and tried to block it all out. After a while, I felt my arm being shaken. I looked up at Donald, who said we were leaving. I wiped my eyes and followed the two of them through the woods. We doubled back the way we'd come, but at a fork we went in a different direction. We left the woods and crossed a cornfield. I had to run between the cornstalks to keep up with them. The sun was still shining but I felt as if the day was gray and miserable.

Outside of a barn, Franklin grabbed me. "You make a sound and I'll kill you."

He lifted me up and carried me through the door. Donald tagged along. We climbed up a ladder. Franklin could easily climb and hold me at the same time. Donald climbed after us. Franklin stopped at a platform at the top of the barn. There was a plank from the platform across the open space to another small platform on the other side. Franklin put me on the plank. I could barely stand on it without falling, but he held me there.

"Walk the plank," he said.

I began to scream, and Franklin smacked me. I gasped and tried not to look down or cry out again.

"Now you listen," he said, "I'll let you off now, but if you ever say anything about what happened today, I'll get you. I'll bring you right back here and make you walk across that plank." I was crying, but as quietly as I could. He carried me back down the ladder.

"Take him home," he told Donald.

Donald took my hand and we walked down the dirt road from the barn. Franklin watched us go. When we got to the main road, I realized we were close to home. I thought it was all right to finally speak.

"Why didn't you do something to help me?" I asked Donald. He didn't answer for the longest time.

Finally, he said, "You wanted to come, and besides, I got back at him."

"How?"

"I made wee-wee in his mouth," he replied proudly.

I think that was the moment when I lost faith in my brother. I saw that he had been as afraid of Franklin as I had been. I always thought that he would take care of me, but now I knew that he wouldn't. He had made no attempt to put his arms around me or comfort me. I was only eight years old, and I'd been terrorized. Yet he had done nothing.

I wouldn't let him see me cry anymore, but I realized for the first time that I was all alone without anyone to help me.

All these years later, I am still able to remember every second of that day. I never discussed it with anyone; I didn't even bring it up again with Donald. It had struck me one day that perhaps something had been going on between Franklin and my brother. After all, Donald was thirteen—did he have an orgasm that day? I wouldn't ever know. I just never trusted him again.

Several years later, I did hear my father say that he'd read that Franklin Pease was dead. He had evidently rested his shotgun against his legs, and it went off, killing him instantly. Even knowing that he was gone, I could never tell anyone about it. But I wondered now, as I lay wide awake beside Roger, if that episode, that was so horrifying at the time, stayed in my subconscious and led me, in some way, to want to kiss Roger's body? If anything, it should have left me with the opposite feeling. Maybe even revulsion. But what I had felt toward Roger was love. It just seemed so natural when it was done out of love. I knew I couldn't tell Roger any of this now. But sometime, soon, as we became more trusting of each other, I hoped I could.

Chapter 19

In the morning, as soon as I was dressed, I managed to slip out of Roger's house without anyone seeing me. He had acted as if nothing had gone wrong the night before and I didn't mention it. My father was picking me up the next morning, so Roger had said we should spend my last night together. He had a business dinner but would come by the shop afterward. I still couldn't shake the feeling that something was wrong between us.

The day went by quickly. Quite a few people came into the shop, and I managed to take in seventeen dollars. I had bought a tiny antique pitcher for Mrs. Goodell as a parting gift and I took it over to her. She told me her gift to me was to be a picnic on a boat she'd rented, a week from Sunday. I could ask anyone I wanted. I said, of course, Liz and Jim, and maybe Roger if he was around. I watched Mrs. Goodell carefully, but she didn't seem to react in any way to Roger's name, so I felt it would be all right.

"I have to get somebody to drive me back, but somehow I'll get here." I said goodbye to her and Liz and told them I was determined to return in ten days for the sailing.

Roger arrived at the shop shortly after nine. He helped me lock up and we started to go to his car. He stopped and said, "I don't think we should go to my room. The Smiths have seen you there too much. Let's just take a walk."

I tried to hide my disappointment at not being alone, but then I had an idea. "Why don't we go up to High Fields?" I asked him. "It's a great place to walk and nobody's ever there."

He said okay and we set out. The moon was almost full, so we had no trouble finding our way. We turned right at the meat market, crossed the railroad tracks and went into the woods. The place was once a huge estate, but now it was a health center. Only the main building was occupied. The paths that wound through the trees were no longer used, so they were overgrown with weeds. I often walked there and had never seen anyone. I took him my favorite way, past the huge totem pole that I guess was brought from Alaska, to the gardener's shed that had been built to look like an English cottage. There was a walled garden, now mostly weeds, and a broken-down stonewall where we were able to sit. We were quiet as we looked into the woods. Shafts of moonlight broke through the leaves and the last of the summer fireflies signaled to each other in the darkness.

"What are we going to do?" I asked. "How will we see each other?"

"I'll come up to Boston every week or so, and we'll go to a museum or a show."

"But how can we be alone?" I was afraid I sounded desperate, but I had to know.

"Don't worry. We'll find a way." He put his arms around me. Even though I knew no one ever came there at night, I was afraid someone might see us. But as he began kissing me, I forgot my fear. I grew terribly excited, and he did too. We started to touch each other and, before we knew it, both of us were spent. He took out his handkerchief and dried us off.

"There," he said. "Do you feel better now?"

"Yes." But I thought it was such an odd thing to say about making love.

When we got back to the shop where Roger's car was parked, I insisted on driving with him to his house. "Please, let me stay with you a few more minutes," I said, hoping I could somehow get him to discuss what our future would be. We drove to Pin Oak Way and got out of the car.

"I'll go back through the fields," I said. "Just come with me to the edge of the grass." We stopped under an arbor studded with late roses. "Please, just tell me it will be all right."

There was a rustle in the grass and Mr. Smith appeared with his dog. "I was just taking a walk," he said, "I hope I didn't startle you."

"Not at all," Roger said. "Alan was just leaving."

"Goodnight," I said, hesitating for a moment, hoping he would ask me to stay.

"I'll go back to the house with you," Roger said to Mr. Smith. Then he turned to me. "Goodnight, Alan," he said and they both walked away. I wanted to call him back, but I knew I couldn't.

In the morning I opened the shop as usual. The only thing that I did differently was that I didn't put the baskets out on the sidewalk. I knew once I was gone, Nana couldn't possibly carry them all in. The cut glass decanter that I'd asked Nana for hadn't sold, so according to our deal, it was mine. I wrapped it very carefully in newspapers and taped it all together. I felt it was my good omen. It was telling me that somehow, I would get to New York. And now, I would be there with Roger.

I walked around the tables in the shop. Even though a lot had sold during the summer, there was still a great deal of merchandise. I guessed Nana would try and sell it all next summer, if she was well enough to have the shop again.

My father would never arrive before noon, so at least I had a few hours left. I had to see Roger one more time. Everything was so undecided between us. If he would just say something to me, at least tell me that he cared for me, I'd be able to go home to Brookline and not worry so much. I knew he'd be angry if I bothered him at work, but I just had to see him. I thought, *I'll just go by and maybe he'll be in the office. I'll just look through the window. I won't even let him know that I'm there.*

I locked the doors of the shop and got on my bike. When I reached the landscaping office that adjoined the nursery, I decided to take my chances. I put my bicycle against a tree and walked in the front door. The room was filled with desks, drafting tables and files. There were blueprints tacked on all the walls. Roger, in his shirtsleeves, was pasting down some cardboard trees on a model.

"Hi." Roger said, "How are you?"

"Fine," I said. "Are you busy?"

He stood up. "No, I can take a break." He led me outside, and we stood under the trees. "Is anything wrong?"

I was careful to keep my voice down. "Please don't be angry that I came."

"Of course not."

"I just had to see you. I thought we'd get things straightened out last night, but Mr. Smith ruined it."

He lit a cigarette. "Everything's all right. I'll come and see you as often as I can, and I'll write you. I promise."

I had planned to surprise him later with the boat trip Mrs. Goodell was arranging, but I decided to tell him now that I'd be back a week from Sunday.

"That's wonderful," he said. His dazzling smile told me what I had wanted to know.

I confessed that Mrs. Goodell had acted suspiciously about our friendship. He shrugged it off and said he'd go by Mrs. G.'s shop, introduce himself, and even ask Liz to dinner.

"That's great, but don't do too much," I said pretending to be jealous. We smiled at each other.

"I've got to go back." He looked straight into my eyes. "I'll miss you very much," he said and then walked back into his office.

I rode back to the store thinking I was the luckiest guy in the world.

Chapter 20

I sat at the desk in the corner of my bedroom in Brookline. It was jammed against the closet wall. There was barely enough room for a chair between it and the windowsill. I had abandoned my old diary because it was too small. Now that I was going to have so much to write about, I had bought a copybook. I planned to fill out one of the pages every day.

So, I wrote *September 8, 1941* on the top line to the left and *Monday* on the right. I had a lot on my mind, but I knew I had to be careful in case somebody found the book and read it. I was going to try to only hint at things. That way, I would remember everything when I looked at the entries, but nobody else would understand them.

So, I began my entry for the day:

Today, at long last, school began.

Spanish (Miss Grant)

English (Mr. Harvey)

Physics (Mr. Warren)

History (Miss Love)

I am a senior taking all fourth-year subjects. Walked to and from school with Nancy Williams. We have come to a perfect understanding. We realize that we enjoy each other's company and that is all. Found my first letter from Roger when I got home. It was a wonderful one. Washed windows for Mother yesterday and she bought me the record, "Tonight We Love," the modern version of Tchaikovsky's Piano Concerto. Roger has the classical version. But it costs too much, so I'm making do with this one that only cost thirty-five cents. It brings back old memories. Also spent ten cents for needles. Mother had two mahjong games today. After dinner, I started to read The Picture of Dorian Gray by Oscar Wilde (220 pages). I am reading it aloud as the writing has much philosophical and psychological background. At first it tells of the great love two men can have for each other. "Close to home." Then Dorian Gray, the most beautiful man, wrecks his life by sin and kills himself when he realizes what he really is. Mother says I can't go to the Cape this weekend for Mrs. Goodell's sailboat picnic, but I can still hope.

I closed the book and hid it under a stack of other books and papers. Since my return to Brookline, I felt like a different person. I saw my old friend Irving and we talked about our vacations, but I had a secret I couldn't tell him. I read Roger's letter over and over. It was short and in it he told me about taking Liz, from Mrs. Goodell's dress shop, to dinner. He said that Falmouth seemed empty now, and he signed it, "Love." I hid it in the back of the clipper ship on the wall along with my nude pictures. I took it out whenever there was no one around. It was on blue stationery and the writing was very neat, almost like printing. A new ice cream parlor opened across the street. Whenever I could make a little money polishing the brass or some other chore, I sat at the counter, had a thick chocolate malted, and thought about Roger.

The days before Mrs. Goodell's sailing party were filled with school, homework, and repeated pleas to be allowed to go. "After all," I argued, "Mrs. Goodell is doing it all for me." The problem seemed to be that someone would have to drive me to the Cape. My father flatly refused to make the trip so soon after taking me home. I managed to bring it up in every conversation and it was gradually driving my parents mad. Suddenly, my brother, who had dropped by to say hello and never paid any attention to me, said he'd take me. He had the day off and thought he'd like to go sailing himself and get some sun. I hated the thought of being with him for two hours on the drive, but I would have done anything to see Roger.

When Sunday came, my parents decided that they would go to Falmouth, too. I kept hurrying everybody up for fear the boat would leave without me. After two hours of driving, my stomach knotted with anxiety. When we reached the dock, Mrs. Goodell and Jim were waiting for me, but no Roger. I began to panic and feel the day was wasted until Roger's car drove up. It was only when he got out, with Liz and a good-looking man in his middle twenties, that I realized what I should have known all along—there was no way I was going to be alone with him that day.

We all piled out of our cars, and kisses and hellos were exchanged. Roger and I shook hands formally. Liz introduced the young man as Randy Witherall whom, she said, she had taught in Boston.

"You'd better say what you taught me," Randy said with a slight leer.

"Interior decorating," Liz emphasized the words, "though I could have taught you a lot more."

"It's never too late," Randy countered.

"In your case," Liz said, "I think it is."

Everyone laughed and we all felt that we were off to a fun day.

"Alan," Liz said to me, "I hope you don't mind my asking Randy. I know it's your party, but Mrs. Goodell said she thought it would be all right."

"Of course," I said.

As we all started to board the boat, Mrs. Goodell asked my mother and father to come along, but they said that they had to be with my grandmother. We watched Dad's Willys pull out of the parking lot and we all waved goodbye.

The boat was named the Hiawatha. The captain, a leathery man in his forties, was never without a cigarette hanging out of his mouth. Like a typical Cape Codder, he never said very much. Mrs. Goodell had asked Connie, who was now engaged to Lester, the fireman. He had come with her and watched her possessively as she grabbed me, mussed my hair and covered me with kisses. When we were all settled, the captain pulled up the gangplank, untied the ropes, and started the motor. As soon as we got out past the jetty, Jim and Mrs. Goodell started serving drinks and lobster rolls.

The sea got very rough when we left the protection of the harbor. The sun was bright, but a strong wind came from the south. It pushed the waves up as high as the railings. There was hilarious laughter whenever somebody got wet. The food hampers began to slide about the deck. I looked around. My brother and Jim were talking to the captain, Connie was snuggled up to Lester, Mrs. Goodell was being fussed over by Randy, and Liz was leaning against Roger, putting food in his mouth. Everyone was having fun except me.

I went as far forward as I could. The sails had been unfurled and the boat dipped up and down, forcing me to hang on with every step I took. I looked for the Vineyard, but I didn't see it. I just stared out at nothing hoping that at any minute Roger would come up beside me. I began to feel sorry for myself. Tears were forming in the corner of my eyes. This was supposed to be a party for me, but nobody seemed to remember that. Even Roger was not paying the least bit of attention to me. I was facing the fact that I was just fifteen years old and they were all grownups who treated me as a kid. I wished I hadn't come.

By the time we docked at Oak Bluffs, everyone was a little drunk. The bobbing of the boat had made them all somewhat seasick, so they had remedied it by drinking more and more. Liz had trouble walking. She kept yelling out a limerick over and over:

"There was a young miss from Cape Cod,

Who thought babies came from God,

T'was not the Almighty,

Who lifted her nightie;

T'was Roger, the lodger,

The sod."

After coffee and cake in a tourist joint on the harbor, we all walked back to the boat arm in arm. I managed to be next to Roger. All he said to me was, "How's school?"

"Fine," I answered. It upset me that he only thought of me as a schoolboy.

Roger turned back to Liz, who kissed him. He returned her kiss, so I lagged behind. I didn't want to watch them. Mrs. Goodell caught up with me. "I was wrong about Roger," she whispered. "He and Liz seem to be getting quite serious."

I could feel my face burn, but I forced a smile to hide a pang of jealousy. I saw Randy walking along up ahead, so I hurried to join him. I thought I would get even with Roger by making him jealous. "Did you catch anything?" I asked Randy, who had been fishing most of the way over.

"Just a small scup. I threw it back."

"Do you live in Boston?" I asked in what I thought was my most winning way.

"On Beacon Hill."

"Oh, I've been there. I went one Christmas Eve to hear the caroling in Louisberg Square. It was beautiful."

"I live just a block over from the square. At least I will when I get out of the Army."

"When will that be?" I asked as if I had a personal interest in it.

"Another couple of months," he said, "if all is well."

"I'm going to live in New York when I get out of school."

"Oh well, that's a very exciting city," Randy replied politely but without much interest.

"I went there once to visit my uncle and aunt. They have a penthouse at the Parc Vendome, and you can see the whole city from their terrace." I looked back to see if Roger was watching me. Liz had sat down on a bench and he was trying to coax her to get up.

"How old are you?" Randy asked.

"I'll be sixteen in a few months."

"We'd better get on the boat."

The trip back was even rougher. At first, everyone sang old songs and laughed. Gradually the sun and the salt spray and the liquor made them all tired. Mrs. Goodell took off her shoes, put her feet up on a deck chair, and fell fast asleep. Connie and Lester, who had kept to themselves, cuddled below in the cabin out of the wind. Roger sat next to Liz on a bench with her head against his chest. My brother had hit it off with Jim and they were trading baseball statistics. I hung around Randy hoping to make Roger jealous, but Randy couldn't seem to think of much to say to me. I wasn't much help. I tried to be sophisticated and grown up. I just didn't know how to make conversation on an adult level. I was way out of my depth and relieved when we docked at Woods Hole.

The group that had been so fresh and eager a few hours before was now wet and tired; our skin burned from too much sun. Roger had a difficult time helping Liz down the gangplank. He had to hold her around the waist to keep her from falling into the water. Finally, he got her on land and set her down on a bench.

"You stay right here," he said to her. "I'm going to get the car." Her eyes opened and closed, and she had a silly smile on her face, as if she didn't know where she was.

"Alan," Roger called to me. "Want to walk to the car with me?"

"Sure," I said as I hurried to catch up to him.

We went across the dock to the parking space. When we were far enough away from the others so that they couldn't hear, he said, "How are you?"

"Awful," I answered.

"So am I." Roger looked past me into the distance.

"You are?" I asked, not looking at him so no one would think that we were having a serious conversation.

"Don't you think I want to be alone with you?" he said. "This trip has been a nightmare!"

"But you seemed so happy with Liz."

"Come on, you asked me to pay attention to her. She's a drunk."

"So, you didn't have a good time?"

"Of course not. I only came to see you."

I felt ashamed. "I'm so sorry," I said. "I got so jealous, I flirted with Randy to make you pay some attention to me."

"I didn't notice," he said.

I felt rather hurt for a minute, but then I was glad Roger hadn't been annoyed.

"We better go back," he said. "I'll come up to Boston the Sunday after next."

"Can't you come sooner?"

"No, I have to work next Sunday. But we'll have a wonderful day. There's an exhibit I want to see at the museum."

"But what are we going to do?" I asked. "I had hoped we could get something settled about our future when I saw you today."

"We'll talk about it then. Now cheer up." He hit me gently on the arm. "Everyone will wonder what's the matter with you."

Roger drove my brother and me to the store. The three of us were jammed in the front seat while Liz slept soundly in the back. When I got out, I managed one mournful look at him that Donald couldn't see. I called to my parents to come out and say hello. When Roger told them that he was planning a trip to Boston, Mother insisted he come to Sunday dinner. Then we all waved as he drove off. Everything was ready for us to leave, and my father hurried us along.

"It'll be midnight before we get home," he warned to speed us up.

I was feeling so happy that I even kissed Nana on the cheek as I said goodbye. She was rather startled. But now everything was going to be all right.

Chapter 21

My mother got me out of bed early. There was a lot to do. She seemed more excited than I was, and immediately assigned tasks that would take the whole morning. Even the samovar had to be polished. The best silver was laid out on a stiff white cloth that hung down over the dining room table. Dad kept out of the way and found a spot far from of the line of action to read the Sunday paper. Donald, who was home for the day, pitched in. By noon, everything was ready for Roger's arrival.

I looked at our apartment as if I were seeing it for the first time, through Roger's eyes. The Japanese prints were beautiful, and I knew some of the antiques were valuable. Maybe he wouldn't notice that the drapes in the living room windows were too short, and the pieces of carpeting that were supposed to go wall to wall didn't quite make it.

It was still warm, with just a hint of fall in the air. Roger arrived wearing a tweed sports jacket with a blue sweater under it. Everyone greeted him as if he were an old friend. No one would have guessed that he was closer to me than anyone else in the family.

The dining room was crowded with furniture. In addition to the table, there was a sideboard and a glass china cupboard filled with polished silver bowls and platters. Mother had outdone herself as she served fruit cup, chicken, four vegetables and a Jell-O mold. Her famous apple pie with ice cream was the dessert. She kept encouraging Roger to eat more and more. He won her over completely with his praise of her cooking.

Dad, busy with his vegetarian food, must have felt left out. He held out a plate to Roger. "I want you to try some of this," he said. "You'll like it."

"Please, Dad, don't make him eat any of that stuff," I said.

"It won't hurt him." He held the plate out again to Roger. "Go ahead, just a taste."

Roger stuck his fork into a substance he had certainly never seen before. "Ha, not bad," he said.

"Doesn't it have a meat flavor?" my father asked.

"Well..." Roger sounded amused.

"If you closed your eyes, and you didn't know, you'd think it was hamburger, wouldn't you?"

"Ralph, please!" my mother interjected.

"Is it really all soybeans?" Roger asked as he smiled at me.

My father was encouraged and said, "Have you ever heard of Doctor Jackson?"

"Dad, don't." I tried to stop him.

"No," my father replied, "Roger's interested. Doctor Jackson only eats soybeans, and at seventy-five, he can lie with his head on one chair and his feet on another, and three women can sit across his chest."

"Well," Roger said with a deadpan face, "I guess at seventy-five, you can't be too particular."

Mother let out a shriek and laughed until tears ran down her plump cheeks. Donald and I joined in. Finally, my father, having obviously decided that he wasn't being made fun of, laughed as well.

"Oh dear," Mother said, getting control of herself, "I haven't laughed so hard for a long time."

"I'll give you Doctor Jackson's book," my father said to Roger. "I think you'll find it interesting."

"I'd like to read it," Roger replied. "Oh, by the way, on Columbus Day weekend, I thought I'd drive up north and see my mother and look at the autumn leaves. I wondered if Alan would like to come along?"

"Oh, that would be great," I said.

"Well," my father answered, "we're not quite sure of our plans yet."

"Is there a chance you all could come?" Roger asked. "I know my mother would love to meet you."

"Oh no," Mother said, "Donald has too much studying to do, and unfortunately I can't possibly get away."

I knew she probably had six mahjong games planned since it was a holiday weekend. I turned to my father. "Can I go?"

"We'll see," he said. I knew from his tone that the chances were good.

After dinner, Donald washed the dishes and I dried them. Mother was on the phone arranging a bridge game for later in the day. Roger and my father were in the living room discussing the possibility of our getting into the war. Roger was over the draft age, but he said he was sure he'd be taken if America got involved. My father was concerned that Donald might not be allowed to finish college. There had been some talk of him enlisting in the Coast Guard.

I kept trying to hear what Roger was saying, but the telephone table was just beyond the kitchen, so Mother's voice dominated the others. I did hear her say on the phone that she and my father "would be there in half an hour," so I assumed she'd found another couple for bridge. My father played too when forced into it. Donald told me that he was going over to a friend's house to study. Suddenly, everybody was saying goodbye, leaving Roger and me alone in the apartment.

We sat awkwardly for a few minutes, making small talk but really listening to see if anyone was coming back up the stairs. When we felt enough time had gone by and no one was returning, we went down the hall to my bedroom. It had been so long since we'd been together physically. We lay on my bed hugging and kissing. Then we touched each other in the way Roger had taught me. The excitement was intense, but what really mattered to me was the feeling of being loved.

Later in the day, we went to the museum, and it was a revelation. A world was opened up to me that I had dreamed of but been afraid to explore alone. Roger was the perfect guide. He made me feel comfortable with art for the first time.

"Don't look at the name under the painting to see if it's by somebody famous," he said. "If you do that, you'll make up your mind to like it because you're supposed to." I smiled guiltily. It was what I always did. "Just look at the painting, and say to yourself, 'Do I like this? What do I feel about it no matter what anybody else says?'"

"I like *that*," I said, as I looked at a large painting in bright colors of South Sea natives in front of an idol. Then I sneaked a look at the name underneath that said Gauguin. "And it is by somebody famous." We both laughed.

Afterward, we sat on a bench in the Fenway, looking at the river. I was feeling sad at the thought of Roger leaving me to drive back to Falmouth. I wanted to talk about our future, but he put me off.

"You're not even sixteen," he said. "You have your whole life ahead of you."

"But I know what I want to do. When I graduate in June, I'm going to be an actor. Either I'll go to New York to study and we'll live there, or I'll study in Boston and we can be together here."

He didn't say anything for a moment. He seemed to be concentrating on two sculls on the river racing toward Harvard. He turned to me. "You know how much older I am than you."

"What difference does that make?" I didn't wait for an answer. "I'm really older than you. I stared at you on the beach until I made you come and talk to me. I got Mrs. Goodell to have the boat trip so I could see you—"

"All right," Roger said. "You're older."

"Good. That's settled." Then I said with great confidence, "Now I make all the decisions. We live together and I'll let you know if it's Boston or New York."

He smiled and got up from the bench. "It's getting late. I have to drive you home."

Chapter 22

Roger had to work half a day on Saturday of the Columbus Day weekend, so he didn't get to Brookline until late in the afternoon. I was busy most of the day packing and unpacking a small suitcase Donald had lent me. I went back and forth to my mother, in her bedroom and in the kitchen, asking her what to take. She was getting exasperated. When I began to bother her about what I should wear, she'd obviously had enough.

"Wear your sky-blue pink," she snapped. It was what she always told me when I couldn't make up my mind what to wear.

"Oh, Mother," I groaned and went back to my room. I looked at my clothes. I hated them all. Anyone would know they were from Filene's basement. Once a year, my mother dragged me to a sale where every suit was eleven dollars. She managed to fit me into one, whether it was a bilious green or an orange plaid. Usually they were all the rejects the good stores hadn't been able to sell. I finally settled on a salt-and-pepper tweed that looked good enough. I figured at least I wouldn't have to wear the ill-fitting jacket in the car.

Roger came up to say hello to my parents, but they hurried us on our way. They were afraid of us driving in the dark. I grabbed my suitcase and winter coat and ran down the stairs. Once we were in the car, Roger reached over and squeezed my arm. "I can't believe they let you come," he said.

We drove north. The day was gray and surprisingly cold for so early in October. There was a lot of traffic as we headed toward Concord. We ran into a crowd leaving a football game and were stalled for a quarter of an hour. We drove through flat farmland that looked like the fields in Kansas that I'd seen when we visited my mother's family.

It was pitch dark when we arrived at Roger's house. We turned into a long driveway and there, right on the highway, was a white-frame farmhouse. It set back quite a way, and there was a bright light on a pole in front of it. It was the only thing lit up for miles. It looked fake to me, almost like a stage set. I couldn't believe that anyone lived there. As the car lights struck the land around the house, I could see the stubble of cornfields. There wasn't a tree around, and everything about it was cold and uninviting.

Roger parked the car near a small, covered porch. Instantly, a light went on above a doorway and a woman came out. She had white hair gathered in a bun, and even in the sketchy light, I could see her resemblance to Roger. She held the front of a cardigan sweater together to keep out the cold.

Roger yelled to her, "Go back inside, Ma. We'll be right in."

We unloaded our two small cases and went into the kitchen. The floor was covered with linoleum, and there was an oilcloth-topped table in the middle with four wooden chairs stained a dark brown. The huge stove still had the old-fashioned iron covers that could be lifted off to put in wood or coal. The overhead light bounced off the shiny pale green walls. I felt like I was inside a huge meat refrigerator.

Roger kissed his mother on the cheek and then introduced me. She made no move toward me and there was no welcoming smile.

"Pleased to meet you," she said. There was nothing unfriendly in her greeting, but I felt I shouldn't be there.

"I'm sorry we're so late," he said, "but we ran into terrible traffic."

"Your brother's been waiting to eat with you, so I'll just give him a call," she said as she started out onto the porch.

Through the window, I could see her pull at a large bell hanging from a rafter. It sounded three times and she came back inside. The table was set, and she told us to wash our hands in the stone kitchen sink. She gave us a thin, worn face towel to share.

Roger's brother didn't look like him at all. He was wearing overalls and must have weighed two hundred pounds. He shook hands with Roger, acknowledged me, and used the same towel after he'd washed his hands. We sat down and their mother put food in front of us. She leaned against the stove and watched us eat.

The supper was tasteless. I wasn't sure if it was chicken or beef stew. It was runny, almost like a soup. There was little conversation. Roger asked questions about the cows and the milking. His brother answered in monosyllables. His mother questioned Roger about his draft status, his work, and if he was keeping company with anyone. I felt acutely uncomfortable. Roger's brother stole little looks at me and seemed to be smirking. I was sure he knew about us.

After a piece of apple pie with a thick crust that tasted of lard, Roger's brother went back to the barn. I asked if I could help with the dishes. Roger said we both would. His mother washed them while we dried and put them back in the cupboards that ran along one side of the room.

"You have nice manners for a young boy," Roger's mother said to me.

"He does, Ma, and you have no idea how smart he is. He was a salesman in his grandmother's shop all summer, and he sold more than she did."

"No, I didn't," I said.

"Don't listen to him," Roger said, "he's just being modest. He's going to be an actor."

His mother was scraping garbage into the pail under the sink. "Is that right?" she said without much interest.

"You should hear him sing," he went on as if he was selling a product.

"Please," I said.

"Why don't you sing that 'Jenny' thing?"

I had seen Gertrude Lawrence in *Lady in the Dark* in Boston and managed to learn one of her songs. "Your mother doesn't want to hear that," I said, hoping that he would stop.

"Sure, she does, come on."

"I just don't feel like it."

"We insist, don't we, Ma?" His mother didn't say anything. She just kept washing the last few dishes.

The idea of singing a song with so many verses, in a brightly lit kitchen to a woman who didn't want to hear it made me try one more time to get out of it. "It's just too long -."

Roger suddenly got annoyed. "Then sing something else. What about that folk song you learned in school where you play two parts? If you're going to be a performer, you're going to have to perform whether you like it or not. Now come on, don't be a baby. Do you want us to coax you?"

"All right, but it's pretty long too."

I propped myself up against the stove. Roger held on with both hands to a chair at the table. His mother still busied herself at the sink, ignoring the argument. I began to sing but my nervousness was making me sound slightly off key. The overhead light drained me of any life. The song, that was meant to be humorous, became a dirge:

On yonder hill there stands a creature
Who she is I do not know;
I'll go ask her hand in marriage
She must answer yes or no.
O no, John! No, John! No, John! No!

I stopped, pretending I'd come to the end. The old woman watched me now but with no expression on her face at all.

"Go on," Roger said.

I took a deep breath and started again.

My father was a Spanish captain
Went to sea a month ago;
First he kissed me then he left me
Bid me always answer no.
O no, John! No, John! No, John! No!

I looked at Roger pleadingly. "That's enough," I said.

"No, it's not," he said firmly. "We want to hear it all."

I felt trapped, but I didn't know what else to do, so I sang on:

O Madam in your face is beauty,

On your lips red roses grow,

Will you take me for your husband?

Madam answer yes or no.

O no, John. No, John. No, John. No!

I stopped, but before I could take a breath, Roger said, "Go on!"

O Madam since you are so cruel,

And that you do scorn me so,

If I may not be your husband,

Madam will you let me go?

O no, John! No, John! No, John. No!

I looked at Roger, whose hands were clenched on the back of the chair. "Can I please skip to the end?"

Roger turned to his mother. "I don't know what's the matter with him. He's never shy. All right, do the last verse."

I sang as quickly as I could:

O hark! I hear the church bells ringing,

Will you come and be my wife?

Or, dear Madam have you settled

To live single all your life?

O no, John! No, John! No. John! No!

I held the last note as long as I could. The room was absolutely still for a moment. I could hear the ticking of a clock from the hall. Then Roger applauded three times and his mother slapped her hands gently without making any sound. The contest was over, and it was clear to me Roger had won.

He led me out of the kitchen into the dark hallway with its forty-five-degree stairway. Once we were away from the stove, it was very cold. We hurried to get to Roger's room. All the walls were white and there wasn't even a picture to cheer them up. I could see into the living room as I walked up the stairs. It was as drab as the rest of the house. I wondered how Roger could have come from this atmosphere. But when I walked into his room, I understood. He turned on the light and I was almost blinded by the color that had been missing everywhere else. The room itself was as white as the others, but shelves had been built in the three windows facing the bed. On the shelves were dozens of dazzlingly colored bottles—red, yellow, blue, amber, green. It was such a relief from the dingy, dull monotony of the rest of the house. I felt I had stumbled on a cache of precious jewels.

"How beautiful they are," I said.

Roger dismissed them. "They're just old bottles I found in junk yards when I was a kid."

We undressed quickly. There had not even been any discussion of my having my own room. I was grateful. Even if he was annoyed with me, at least I would be warm sleeping next to him.

When we were in the iron bed that was painted white like the walls, I said, "I'm sorry."

He had his back to me. "What for?"

"I sang so badly."

"Don't be silly. You were fine. I don't know what you made such a fuss about."

I waited but Roger didn't say anything more. "Are you angry?"

"No, why should I be angry?"

I started to get really alarmed. "Did I do something wrong?"

"Don't be childish. Go to sleep."

I put my hand on his shoulder. "Please, tell me, what's the matter?"

Roger turned away and muttered, "It's all hopeless. Go to sleep."

Chapter 23

As we drove north, the leaves were glorious but neither of us was able to enjoy them. Roger's mind was somewhere else, and I was afraid to intrude. I wanted to talk about his mother and his brother, but everything I said seemed to antagonize him. I felt as if I were walking on eggshells. We somehow got through the day with an occasional "Look at that maple," or "My God, that orange color is incredible." To make matters worse, we even managed to find the most dismal roadside stand for lunch.

While he drove, I studied the map and tried to find a place for us to spend the night. "What about Bellows Falls," I asked, having found a name on the map in larger letters than the towns around it. "It must be big enough to have rooming houses."

"Fellow's balls," Roger said, smiling for the first time that day. "Perfect, we'll stay at Fellow's Balls."

The town was much farther than it had looked on the map. We were exhausted by the time we got there. We found a place to stay and were sent nearby to get soup and a sandwich. Everything else was closed on Sunday. I tried to get Roger to say what was bothering him, but there was no response.

"I wish I could help you drive," I said. "I don't think you're having much fun."

"Don't be silly. I'm having a great time."

The room had twin beds. It was damp and colorless with faded chintz slip-covered chairs, an ugly stained oriental rug, and curtains at the windows that had yellowed with all the washing that I was sure never made them clean. Over each headboard was a hanging lamp with most of its fringe missing, giving it a cockeyed look. When I was in bed, I decided to get things straight.

"What have I done?" I asked.

"What do you mean?" Roger answered as I knew he would.

"You know. Please tell me."

"Nothing."

"If I only knew what I'd done to upset you, I'd apologize, But I don't know what it is."

"You haven't done anything," Roger said as he continued to undress.

"I'm so miserable. Please tell me." I started to cry. I had looked so forward to this trip and it had turned out to be a series of mistakes.

"Now don't behave like a little boy," he said.

"But you're acting like I'm the last person in the world you want to be with." I somehow stopped my tears. "I thought we loved each other."

"Let's not discuss it."

I steeled myself. "Do you love me?"

"That has nothing to do with it."

"Well then what is it? It's so awful. I don't know what to do—"

"Alan, you're such a child."

"No, I'm not. Why do you keep saying that?"

"Because you are." He sounded like a kind teacher. "When I first met you on the beach, I thought you were eighteen. Then when I heard your real age, you still seemed so much older. But I have realized on this trip that you're just a little boy who has to be coaxed to get up and sing a song."

"I knew you were angry about my singing, but I just didn't feel like it."

"It's my fault, really. I keep treating you as a grownup. I keep forgetting—"

"I'm grown up enough to love you and want to spend my life with you."

Roger walked over and sat on my bed. "We've got to get something straight. You've got to stop talking about us spending our lives together."

"You don't love me." I was afraid I was going to cry again.

"Alan, I'm twice your age, and we're the same sex."

"It doesn't matter as long as two people love each other," I said.

"Don't be ridiculous," he replied.

"What does the right sex or age have to do with it? Look at my parents, or Mrs. Goodell and Jim. They're the right sexes and the right ages. It doesn't seem to have made them happy."

"Come on, Alan." He sounded like he'd had enough.

"Or my grandmother, or Liz, or Connie. She just wants to get married, so she went out and found Lester." I was trying desperately to make him understand. "They don't love anybody the way I love you, so why can't we be together?"

He sighed and put his hands on his forehead. "Alan, I'm going to ask you something. If you do love me, you have to stop all this. I just can't go through it all the time. He took his hands down and looked straight into my eyes. "I care very much for you, but you've got to stop all this, or you'll kill everything."

I knew I shouldn't say anymore, so I just sat quietly. After a few moments, he reached over and kissed me. "Now, let's go to bed."

I started to get into my bed again, but he took me over to his. Oh God, I thought, I just pray that everything's going to be all right now.

Chapter 24

Once I was back home, I stopped writing in my diary. For one thing, I was afraid somebody might find it and read it. And then I was just so busy with homework that I could never seem to finish. There wasn't much to tell anyway. Roger came up from Falmouth to see me toward the end of October, and we went to a concert at Mrs. Jack Gardner's museum. We sat in the flower-filled courtyard most of the afternoon because my parents were in the apartment and we couldn't go there. We weren't able to be alone, so it turned out to be a frustrating visit.

In November, on my birthday, a package arrived from Roger. It was an etching of people standing on the steps of St. Paul's cathedral in London. There was a note attached: "Not very much, but at least an original Pennell." I hurried to the public library to look up Pennell and discovered that he was a famous American artist. I owned a real work of art. I immediately made plans to get it framed. The next day, another package arrived from Roger. It was a yellow, cashmere sleeveless sweater. I didn't let on to Roger that I liked it better than the etching, but it was perfect to wear with the new Hart, Schaffner and Marx sports jacket my parents had given me. I called to thank Roger, and he told me that he'd be in Brookline the first Sunday in December.

He came up to see me as he had promised. To describe what happened on that day, I had to get out my diary again. I felt I had to keep a record of what was going on because it was just too much to remember. Besides, I felt I owed it to posterity so that the world would know everything when I was gone.

Monday, December 8, 1941

Today is an ominous one to start a journal of my life. President Franklin Roosevelt declared war on Japan at twelve thirty-five p.m.

Of course, there was school, but everyone heard the President because radios had been set up everywhere. The message was short – just 500 words. He summed up the events that happened yesterday...

We were sitting at Sunday dinner when a friend burst in and almost hysterically shouted, "The Naval Base at Pearl Harbor has been bombed by the Japanese!" We turned on the radio and it was confirmed. Roger was here and he, of course, was worried as the age limit will be up to thirty-five again. He is thirty. Everybody was concerned but not worried. It was said constantly that this was suicide by the Japanese. However, everything is changed today. The record will be left for history, but the seriousness of the situation is now being revealed.

Today, the excitement of war was tremendous. I should have said that the President asked Congress to declare war. The vote was unanimous except for one woman. A great deal of damage is being done to our positions, warships, men, etc. So far, Japan is victorious. It has gained Guam and Wake Island. We are getting allies by the hour many South American republics.

I received quite a large part in the high school radio broadcast for Wednesday. I play a rich, handsome young man whose father goes bankrupt, who saves a man from committing suicide, who loves a girl and tells her so   all in fifteen minutes. I also whistle Tchaikovsky's 'Piano Concerto.'

I got a D+ on a physics test today. I'm beginning to worry that I shouldn't have switched to a science curriculum. My Uncle Sumner said I'd have to do that in order to be an architect, but I don't want to be an architect anymore. Especially since Roger has encouraged me to go after my dream of being an actor. I'm getting lousy marks now. I just don't like physics or math. And I was doing so well in my other courses, but it's too late to change.

I can hardly study or do anything with the radio so full of reports. The war is fascinating as well as horrible. The day was very cold. Snowflakes flurried down for a few minutes yesterday. We plan to go to Florida a week from next Friday. Britain declared war on Japan before we did. Many Americans say that Germany forced Japan into war, and that we should declare war on Germany, the true enemy. Farewell Peace."

I put the diary away. I planned to keep track of all the battles until we won the war. But in a few days, it was so complicated I couldn't figure it out anymore. I sat every night at the radio with Mother and Dad. We listened, horrified, to what was going on. I kept worrying about what would happen to Roger. I wished I could tell my parents about my feelings, but it was impossible.

Chapter 25

The trip to the South was a total escape from everything that was going on in my life. The early excitement of the war had calmed down, but we never missed the news reports on the radio. We all listened gravely to the losses. My mother put her tongue against her upper teeth and made clicking sounds of disapproval at every atrocity. We drove to Miami to deposit my grandmother for her winter vacation. I thought the Norwyn Hotel, where we stayed, was very modernistic. I was embarrassed as we stood in the lobby while Mother beat the manager down from three dollars to one dollar a night. However, we congratulated her when we got to the rooms. I had never been in a hotel with a shower and a bathtub that wasn't down the hall.

After a few days, we moved to the Battle Creek Sanitarium, the home of Dad's idol, Doctor Jackson. In return for my father taking pictures of the adobe buildings that were covered with friezes of Indian thunderbirds, we were given free rooms.

The grounds were lush, filled with hibiscus and oleander. I walked around and thought about Roger. We had not had a chance to be alone with all the excitement of Pearl Harbor, but we had managed a moment in which he promised to write me as soon as he knew where he would be. He was leaving Falmouth since there was no more landscaping in December. He was going to look into getting a commission in the Army. The problem was that since I had no idea where we would be staying in Florida, I couldn't get a letter from him until we returned home. I couldn't even write to him since he didn't know where he would be. For weeks, I felt I was in limbo. The people at the sanitarium were all old and it made me miss Roger even more.

The food was vegetarian, so Dad was ecstatic. He savored the menu and insisted on reading it aloud: "meatloaf, turkey or veal stew, chop suey." They were all made with meat substitutes.

"Doesn't it taste just like chop suey?" my father asked exultantly. My mother and I knew we didn't have to answer.

When we returned to Brookline, a letter was waiting for me. I recognized the pale blue envelope and took it to my room where I could read it by myself. It was very formal. We had agreed not to put things in letters that other people might see. Roger wrote that he was going into the Army as an officer and would be in training school. He didn't know where, but he would let me know. At the present time, there was nowhere I could write him. I put the letter in the back of the clipper ship picture with the few others I had. I went to the dresser and opened the drawer where I kept my few sweaters. I touched the yellow cashmere Roger had sent me, thinking it would bring him closer to me. It didn't. The bottle of Old Spice was on the top of the dresser in front of me. I couldn't picture Roger's face. Weeks went by, but there was no word from him.

I was still having problems with physics and math. I just didn't have the aptitude for them. I tried to study, but I felt as if I were in a morass. I didn't know how to get out of it. I looked for ways to avoid the work that made less sense to me as it became more complicated. I did anything to avoid it, spending most of the evening cleaning up my room, getting everything ready so I could study. But by the time I finished the straightening up, I had to go to sleep to be ready for school the next day. So, I was never fully prepared, and I failed one test after another. I began to worry that I wouldn't graduate.

Tryouts were announced for Prize Speaking. I had received honorable mention the year before, but this time I was determined to win. Although the award was supposed to be for excellent speech, I had observed that the winners usually did excerpts from plays in which they could use several different voices to show off their range. I ransacked the library looking for some special material and I stumbled across Stephen Vincent Benet's *The Devil and Daniel Webster*. I counted up the number of characters. There were fourteen. I began to plan the voices I would use. Some would have English accents. Some would sound raspy or wheezy. Daniel Webster, I decided, would sound like an old Victorian actor rolling his R's. I would give the Devil a sibilant S in addition to an insinuating manner.

I was chosen as one of the ten contestants and began to rehearse on my own. I edited the short story to twelve minutes, and I went over it in my head, walking to and from school, driving in the car and even sitting in classes. I woke in the middle of the night and got up, trying not to disturb my parents who were down the hall. I walked into the bathroom, closed the door and stood in front of the mirror. I acted out the whole thing, talking very softly, but as I reached the section where a hanging judge says, "Kill them. Kill them all!" I got carried away and invariably started to talk loudly. My parents had heard me because "Kill them. Kill them all" became a catchphrase at the breakfast table. But at least they didn't complain.

As April approached and the night of Prize Speaking drew near, a letter arrived from Roger. It was just a few lines to say that he was in Officer's Training School in the west and he had no idea when he would be east again. I knew he couldn't write anything personal, but it was so cold, like a duty note sent to a distant relation. At least there was a return address, so I wrote back and told him of my hopes of winning the contest and my continued plans to go to New York to be an actor.

College became a serious subject at the supper table. My parents had always intended that I go to the Massachusetts Institute of Technology to study architecture. Then I would be able to go into my rich uncle's architectural business. D's in physics and math were making them question my chances. Since I was only sixteen, a year younger than my schoolmates after skipping second grade, I asked to stay out of school and work for a year before going on to college. Nothing was settled but as the weeks went by, no college applications were sent out.

The night of Prize Speaking, I took a long bath and scrubbed my body as if preparing for a sacrifice. I felt if I were really clean, I would stand a better chance. I put on the dark blue suit Mother had bought me for Confirmation and brushed down my cowlick. I stood around waiting for my parents to get ready. Even though I was the last one on the program, we all had to be there at seven-thirty, or an alternate would go on. I got more and more nervous as Mother kept changing outfits. She acted as if it were *her* big evening.

Backstage at the school auditorium, the atmosphere was oppressive. All of the contestants sat on a row of wooden chairs as if they were at a wake. Several came up to me and told me they were sure I would win. The day before, at a dress rehearsal, everyone had a chance to see their competition for the first time, since we had rehearsed alone with the drama teacher. My selection was the longest and certainly had the most voices, so I was considered the frontrunner. Each student who said I was good made me more nervous. I had always been taught not to show off, so I said that I wasn't really good and that they were much better. I suddenly thought maybe I'd better lose, rather than agree with their praise of me. I began to feel ill.

Once the program started, we all sat waiting in the semi-darkness at one side of the stage, under the heavy ropes that controlled the lights and the curtain. One by one, someone got up, walked to the wings, paused for a moment to get courage, and then strode out onto the illuminated stage. One girl did an excerpt from *Jane Eyre*. A boy did one from *Cyrano*. Another recited a stirring speech about the glory of America. As each one finished and walked back to the group waiting, he or she was told how wonderful they were by the others. That coupled by the applause made my confidence start to disappear, as if it were sand pouring through an hourglass.

After the intermission, my turn was coming soon. I pretended to be in control, but in my head, I kept going over and over my lines. Since my selection was so much longer than the others, I never got through it completely in my head before someone came off the stage and broke my concentration. I had to start at the beginning again when the next contestant started to speak. I never got to the end and I wasn't sure I remembered it at all. My panic increased when my biggest rival, a fellow with a deep, beautifully modulated voice, came offstage, after doing Daniel Webster's *Prosecution in the Knapp – White Case* to immense applause. Everyone looked uneasily at me as if I had just lost. The girl who was immediately before me got onstage and recited *The Old Lady Shows Her Medals*. She brought the house down with her Irish washerwoman tearjerker.

The audience was still applauding when I went on. I stood in the center of the small living room set and felt the evening was over. I was the last one and it was late. Everyone was tired and obviously the boy and girl winners had been chosen. The lights were very bright and for a moment, I didn't know where I was. Everything stopped like a smashed clock, and then I heard myself speaking: "It's a story they tell in the border country where Massachusetts meets New Hampshire and Vermont." I didn't seem to be there at all. I felt far away. I saw the people in front of me and wondered what they were looking at. I thought at any moment I could just walk off the stage and it would all be over. But my voice kept going on and on while my body was very still. When I began doing the different voices, I relaxed somewhat. I got caught up in the action as the characters spoke to each other.

The people in the audience disappeared. I came down from the ceiling where I had been watching a young boy in a dark blue suit. I began to be the Devil talking to Daniel Webster. The words poured out of me. A part of me sensed that I was taking a long time and there was some restlessness in the audience. But I ignored it and went on to the end. When Evil was defeated and Right had triumphed, I described dawn coming up with the crow of a rooster. And then, it was over, and I walked offstage. I went back and sat in my chair. I barely heard what sounded to me like mild applause. "Very good," someone near me said. But I knew that's what we all had been saying to each other.

The school orchestra played endlessly, awaiting the decision of the judges. All the contestants whispered together, pretending it didn't matter. I walked away from them. It did matter, and I hadn't been as good as I had been in front of the bathroom mirror. I paced back and forth behind the set, wishing it was over so I could go home.

The drama teacher came up to me. She whispered, "Don't worry." She looked to be sure none of the others could hear, "You've won."

"What do you mean?" I asked.

"I was just with the judges," she said. "Don't let on that you know."

She walked away and instead of feeling jubilant I thought, *why did she have to tell me*? Now I have to pretend to be surprised when they make the announcement. I'm going to have to act like I didn't know anything.

I went back and joined the others who were fidgeting, waiting for the judges. They were all saying that they were sure they hadn't won. I said I knew I'd been terrible, but I felt so dishonest. I hated lying to them. Suddenly, we heard the drama teacher's voice announcing that the girl who did *The Old Lady Shows Her Medals* and I had won. We were pushed out onto the stage to a roar of applause. All I could think of was that I had to act like I was just getting the news, but the teacher and I knew what a fake I was. It somehow spoiled the moment. The judges surrounded us to offer their congratulations. One of them took me aside.

"I'm Elliot Norton," he said. "I'm the drama critic of *The Boston Globe*. I just wanted to tell you how talented I think you are."

I muttered, "Thank you."

"You should be an actor," Mr. Norton added.

What he said made the whole experience worthwhile. I forgot about knowing I'd won beforehand. This was the moment I had worked and prayed for.

My parents came backstage and joined the group surrounding me. Mother, in her cloth coat with the fox collar, was all over the place introducing herself as "Alan Schein's mother." She insisted on standing beside me in the pictures the photographers were taking. I couldn't shake the feeling that I'd cheated by knowing that I'd won before they announced it.

When we got out to the car I said, "Where are we going?"

"Home, of course," my father said.

"Aren't we going to celebrate or anything? Can't we just go to St. Claire's for ice cream? A lot of the kids are going."

"It's much too late," my father replied.

We drove home in silence. When we arrived at the apartment, my father stopped the car at the front door to let us out since he parked around the corner.

As I got out, he said, "I thought that boy who did the Knapp-White Case was the best. I thought he should have won."

I didn't say anything. I went upstairs, undressed, and got into bed. I just lay there, thinking about what my father had said. *Why did he say that? Even if he believed it, why would he want to hurt me so and ruin my evening?* All I could think of to do was to somehow get away from him, from all of them.

I had to leave home.

Chapter 26

I took the Sunday paper up to the roof of our apartment. There was a wooden platform with a post at each corner where the tenants hung their laundry. I spread an old towel on the boards and lay down. The sun wasn't very strong, but at least it would give me some color so that I'd look pretty good at graduation the following week. I'd managed to pass the exams even though my mind was on other things. My relationship with my father had grown even more distant since Prize Speaking. Mother, sensing it, became overly affectionate, as if trying to make up for him. I had begun to avoid her sticky kisses and fondling that tried to turn me into a child again. All I kept going over and over was how to get away from this place that I knew was killing me.

I had hoped Roger would be helpful and give me some advice. I had written him about my winning the contest and what the drama critic had said. A short note came back saying he'd always known how talented I was. I'd heard nothing since, although I had written him letter after letter. I figured he must be terribly busy at Officer School and probably had troubles of his own.

As I lay in the sun, I read the front page of *The Boston Globe* and skimmed some of the news inside. Then I turned to the want ads. I had to find something to do for the summer. My grandmother wasn't going to open her store because with rationing, not many people would make it to the Cape. I looked down the long columns of ads. There were so many men being drafted that there were endless jobs, but not for sixteen-year-old boys with no experience. Suddenly I sat up. There was an ad that read: "Actors wanted for Summer Theater. Send picture and resume to Forbes Theater, Rockport, Mass."

It had never occurred to me that actors got work by looking in the classifieds. I gathered up the papers and ran down to the apartment. My parents had gone to visit my uncle and aunt, so I had the place to myself. I got some of my mother's stationery and wrote a letter saying I had won Prize Speaking and the Drama Critic of *The Boston Globe* had said how talented I was. I mentioned some plays I had been in, some radio shows, and that I was just graduating high school. That would make them think I was seventeen instead of sixteen. My father was always taking my picture to try out new lenses or a different kind of film, so I had dozens of pictures to choose from. I picked the one that made me look the oldest. The post office was closed, but I would go first thing in the morning. I hid everything in a bureau drawer so no one would know.

We were having supper several weeks later when the phone rang in the other room. Mother got up and answered it, and said it was for me. A deep, husky voice announced, "This is Marla Forbes and I'm calling in response to your letter."

I took a deep breath. "Oh yes," I said.

"I'm very interested in your picture and background. Can you drive to Rockport next Sunday for an interview?"

"Of course," I said, and we set a time. I was so excited that I rushed back to the kitchen with my news expecting them both to congratulate me on finding such a great opportunity. I'd forgotten for a moment what they were like. The rest of the meal was spent with my mother and father saying that there was no way I was going to summer stock where everyone drank and smoked.

My father got really angry at the prospect and said I was far too young to be with people like that. Mother calmed him down and asked me where the theater was and if I knew who was running it. I replied that it was in Rockport, only an hour and a half away, and the woman who owned it said her name was Marla Forbes.

My father got apoplectic. "I know all about her," he said. "She's the black sheep of one of the best Boston families. Not only that, she's a nightclub singer and a drunk."

I realized I was getting nowhere, so I decided to bring out the grudge list that I hated to resort to. "You never let me do anything," I said. "You never sent me to art school, you never gave me piano lessons, you never gave me anything." I hated to bring these things up because I knew they could never afford classes for me, but I had to make them feel guilty. I stopped for a minute to show them how miserable I was. Then I said, "Just let me go out to see Miss Forbes. Mother can come with me and then we can decide. If it's terrible, I won't go. Anyway, they haven't offered me a job. I would just be going for an interview."

My father agreed to sleep on it, and I fired my last shot. "You've always given Donald anything he wants. You taught him photography, you sent him to college, and you won't even let me have something I got all by myself." I think that's what did it, because on Sunday, my mother and I were on the road going to Rockport.

When we got there, it was pouring rain and the town looked like a wet dog. Most of the shops were still closed at the end of May, and the small deserted beach with the rock jetties in the center of town did nothing to make it more attractive. My mother stopped the car to ask directions to the summer theater. She was told it hadn't opened yet, but we could find the building up a long hill. When we got to the top, we saw a gray shed that looked abandoned nestled in a grove of large white pines. There were broken chairs and several doors lying in the yard. Mother made a disapproving face and said she would wait in the car.

"Get it over with quickly," she said, "because you're certainly not going to spend the summer here."

I ran through the rain up several steps to a platform with two over-sized doors that looked like they'd come from a church. I knocked on one of them and it immediately flew open. A middle-aged woman with a scarf tied around her head rushed out into the yard. She grabbed a police dog that was standing there.

"Get in here, you stupid thing," she said. "I've been looking all over for you." She pulled the dog by its collar onto the platform. "Oh," she said, changing her tone. "I didn't see you. Do you want something?"

"I have an appointment with Miss Forbes," I said. "I'm a little early."

"Then you're Alan," she said sweetly. It was the same deep voice I'd heard on the phone. "I'm Marla. Come on in."

The inside of the building was even more chaotic than the outside. Through the hall and beyond two open doors was the auditorium where most of the folding chairs were lying on their sides. The stage was a mass of rubble and looked as if a bomb had struck it.

"We're just starting to get things in order," Miss Forbes said brightly as she guided me into her office. She cleared off a chair for me to sit on. I looked around, waiting for her to settle. There were clothes and books everywhere. I could see my picture on the desk next to an open can of dog food. A kettle was boiling on an electric two-burner stove, and the steam made the air in the room even more humid.

"Would you like some tea?" Miss Forbes asked, as if we were sitting at the Copley Plaza in Boston.

"No thank you, Miss Forbes," I replied. "My mother is waiting in the car and we have to drive back to town."

"Call me Marla," she said, "everyone does. Now, tell me about yourself."

I went through my entire history that I dragged out as much as I could. It still seemed to be over with much too quickly. Miss Forbes leaned forward on a stool, smoking and listening intently. I thought she was not bad looking, but her hair had been bleached a brassy blond and seemed too long for a woman of her age. It hung down to her shoulders from under a bright red kerchief. She was wearing a rumpled, mustard-colored slack suit yet she somehow seemed quite elegant. When I told her how much I wanted to be an actor, she was very sympathetic.

"I can't promise you anything," she said, "but we'll see what happens. So many boys are going into the service that who knows, maybe something will open up for you."

"Oh, that would be wonderful," I said.

"Yes," she replied. "I just wanted to meet you so I'd know what parts you could be right for. But don't count on anything."

I was afraid she'd only think of me for young roles. "I don't have to play my age," I said suddenly desperate. "In Prize Speaking, I played a lot of old people, too."

"I'm sure," she said kindly. "Let's just see what happens."

She insisted on taking me out to the car. It was still pouring so she grabbed what looked like a beach umbrella and held it over our heads. She helped me into my side of the car and stood waiting to meet my mother. I knew introducing her was going to be a mistake, but I couldn't refuse.

"This is Miss Forbes, Mother," I said, fearing the worst.

Miss Forbes suddenly became the lady of the manor greeting a guest. "Oh, Mrs. Schein," she said. "I'm so happy to meet you. I wish you could come in for some tea on this miserable day, but Alan said you must get back to town. Your son is enchanting and so polite. He's a great credit to you."

Mother smiled her most winning smile. "Thank you so much."

Water was streaming off the umbrella as she stood there. "Well, I mustn't keep you," she said. "Have a safe trip." She reached through the window and clutched my arm. She looked straight into my eyes as if she had something to tell me. She spoke so softly that, with the rain, I couldn't make out what she said.

"I beg your pardon," I said. "I couldn't hear you."

"The rain may pass," she said, as if it had some meaning for me, and then she went back up the stairs waving goodbye. We drove off waving as well. Neither of us said a word on the way home. The whole day wasn't even mentioned at supper.

It was as if it had never happened.

Chapter 27

July was very hot. I spent most of my time on the roof, reading until the heat got unbearable. Then I just wandered around. Everyone I knew had gone to summer camp or was taking courses to get ready for college. I wasn't going to be with them. I'd ended school with three B's, a C, and two D's. It was good enough to graduate but not good enough to get into any decent college. Fortunately, the award for Prize Speaking was given at the graduation ceremony, so I did get to walk up to the podium for my prize. But everyone else I knew won awards for their scholarly achievements, so I felt like an ignominious failure. Every morning, as soon as it was time for the mail delivery, I rushed down the stairs with my key and opened the box. But there was no letter from Roger. After a while, I pretended to myself that I didn't expect one, but it was always in the back of my mind.

I had just come from the library and was carrying my bicycle up the stairs. It was very light but difficult to manipulate around the curve in the wall just before the apartment landing. After I unlocked the door and wheeled it into the hall outside my father's photographic darkroom, I took the books out of the basket on the handlebars and went into the living room. I opened all the windows. The noise from the street and the smell from the three gas stations we overlooked filled the air. But at least there was a slight breeze. I chose a Walter D. Edmonds book   I was fascinated by the rough and tumble world of the Erie Canal. I settled in the wing chair next to the marble-topped table. I suddenly noticed an open telegram next to the lamp. I reached over and picked it up. It was addressed to me. I quickly opened it afraid it was something about Roger. Instead I read, "PLEASE CALL FORBES THEATER IMMEDIATELY ROCKPORT 2301 COLLECT." It was signed "Marla Forbes."

Written across the telegram in Donald's handwriting was a message. He must have been there for a few hours. "Mother said not to call." God, I've got to telephone. But if I do, and Mother said not to, she'll never let me go. Maybe I should take a chance and at least find out what it is. It could be a job. I'd better wait. I got terribly excited. I'd get away from home and be on my own. I suddenly thought, *I'm not going to be a kid anymore.* As if I needed a sign of my new maturity, I remembered where some Pall Mall cigarettes were hidden. I took one out and lit it. I inhaled deeply. I was going to be a grownup and an actor.

When my mother arrived about five, I was ready for her. I didn't even let her change her card game clothes before attacking. "I've got to go," I said. "I don't have a job for the summer; I'd be where it's cool. I can swim and get healthy. I can learn about acting and see if I have any talent. I can find out if it's a life I want while I'm still young enough to do something else. I'm a year younger than all my friends going to college, so just let me have this experience and then I'll do anything you want me to do."

I followed her around her bedroom as she started taking off her clothes. "I want to make money so I can take care of you," I said as she buttoned her housedress. "I want you to have a mink stole like all your friends have. It's not fair that you don't have one, and I'm going to get one for you." I knew I was touching on the one thing that my mother regarded as a symbol of happiness. I said it as if it was just a question of her unwrapping the package.

When my father arrived, it was not so easy. He was dead set against the theater, but suddenly Mother was arguing on my side. "Why don't we at least let him call and find out what it is?" she said. "All of this discussion may be pointless if the woman isn't going to offer Alan a job. Maybe it's just another interview."

"Well..." Dad couldn't think of a good reason to stop it. "All right."

I ran to the phone and dialed. It rang and rang. I kept praying that Miss Forbes was there. I felt my stomach turning over and over. The telegram had been sent early that day. She probably got someone else when she didn't hear from me. But then Miss Forbes answered the phone and her voice was warm and friendly. "Alan," she said, "I need someone immediately. I will pay you fifteen dollars a week. You can get a room in the house where all the actors live for only three dollars and food is very inexpensive. You can live quite well on the money. But I must have a decision right away. Do you want me to talk to your parents?"

I was horrified. That would really ruin it. "No, thank you," I said. "I'll speak to them and call you in the morning."

Donald showed up to have supper and joined in the fray. Of course, he was against me going, but he'd always been opposed to anything I wanted. The five-year difference in our ages had always seemed to prevent us having a close relationship. I knew he resented me growing tall while he stayed so short. He had acne as a kid, so his face was pockmarked, and he was even going bald. People always said nice things about the way I looked, but they didn't compliment him. I was certain I'd always been a thorn in his side. So, it was no surprise that he was against me being an actor.

Mother was serving the rest of the sponge cake she had baked for the girls, as she called the women that she played cards with, when I had an inspiration. "You're always worried about my health," I said to my father, "but you don't mind me spending the summer in the sweltering heat in Brookline, when I could be cool and swimming every day in Rockport."

There was a long silence during which Donald, my mother and I just looked at my father. We all remembered he used the excessive heat to get me to spend the past summer helping my grandmother in her shop. How would he get out of this one?

After what seemed an interminable time, he said, "What about the smoking and the drinking?"

"I won't smoke, and I won't drink," I said firmly.

Dad got up from the table and went to the icebox. He took out a bottle of soy acidophilus milk and walked back to the table. He'd begun wearing his glasses all the time and the reflection of the overhead light kept me from seeing what was in his eyes.

"I'll tell you what," he said. "I'll let you go on one condition—that Mother goes with you."

I was shocked, but I decided to quit while I was ahead. I was going to summer stock and my mother was going with me.

Chapter 28

I couldn't wait to write Roger that at last I was going to be a professional actor, and I was even going to be paid for it. There still had been no letter from him, but I kept convincing myself that he was too busy to even have a minute to write. This news, I was sure, would make him at least dash off a few lines to congratulate me. In my letter to him, I said that my good fortune was mainly due to his encouragement and belief in my talent. I said to send the letter in care of the Forbes Theater in Rockport, so I'd be sure to get it right away.

On Wednesday, my father drove my mother and me to Rockport. He only stayed long enough to help us find a room near the theater. The landlady said she wasn't too keen on "theater folk," but Mother charmed her, and then she admitted we were different. Once we unpacked in the twin-bedded room with its nautical lamps, maple furniture, and white bedspreads covered with tiny balls, we walked into town. It was the height of the tourist season and the narrow streets were jammed. We wandered onto a long jetty, wide enough to have shops on either side that had been made out of fisherman shacks. Mother held my hand as we walked through the crowds. Two older women came toward us and stopped. They stared at us and then one of them said to the other, distastefully, "She looks old enough to be his mother." We both laughed.

In our second phone conversation, Miss Forbes told me that I wouldn't be needed for rehearsal until Thursday morning. She would leave tickets at the box office for the play that was opening. We walked up the long hill to the theater. I caught a quick glimpse of Miss Forbes and waved to her, but she must have been too busy to notice me.

There were just a handful of people in the audience, but at least the theater had been cleaned up. The play was a French farce that was greeted with stony silence. It didn't help matters that the set was flimsy and every time a door slammed to make a comic point the flats tottered precariously. There was a certain excitement in anticipating the disaster that was bound to happen. When it didn't, everyone settled down to an interminable wait for the final curtain. My mother wanted to go backstage, but I dissuaded her. I wanted to keep her away from the actors as long as I could.

I was the first to arrive at the theater the next morning. The front door was unlocked so I walked into almost total darkness. Shutters covered all the windows and I was afraid to turn on the lights. I sat down in the back and waited. After half an hour, people began to arrive, and the lights were turned on. I was embarrassed to be sitting in the dark, so I just stayed where I was. No one noticed me. I recognized all the actors from the night before. Several of them were painfully hung over. The huge police dog came bounding in, pulling Miss Forbes on the other end of the leash. She kissed everyone on both cheeks and then disappeared into her office. She came back without the dog and announced the rehearsal would begin.

"Has anyone seen the new actor?" she asked.

Everyone shrugged and said "No."

"Oh dear," Miss Forbes sounded annoyed. "What'll we do?"

I forced myself to stand up. "Here I am," I said.

"Alan," Miss Forbes called out. "What are you doing there? Come here." I walked to the footlights, feeling everyone's eyes on me. "Welcome," Miss Forbes said warmly. Then she introduced me to the actors. I made mental notes of each one so I wouldn't mix them up.

There were two leading men: Edward   a bookish, tall, pleasant-looking man in his thirties who wore horn-rimmed glasses and sucked on a pipe, and Rusty   a handsome, six foot, husky guy, in his twenties, with a mass of reddish brown hair, a golden tan, a throaty voice and color-coordinated shirt and slacks.

The leading women were Susan—a pretty, slightly pudgy blond in her twenties; and Trilby—a thin, elegant girl, also in her twenties, who was married to Edward and holding a tiny baby.

The character people were: Flo—a small, chubby, plain woman in her forties who wore her hair in a bun and had old-fashioned round glasses pushed down her nose, and Jack—a wiry little man who resembled a jockey and, from the look of his flushed face, drank a lot.

I shook hands with them all and told them how much I had enjoyed the play the night before. They were very welcoming except for Rusty, who walked away from me immediately and sat down to read his script.

"Where are Alan's sides?" Miss Forbes asked into the air. A girl appeared from the office with a small folder that she handed to me. "This is Wendy. She does the sets," Miss Forbes said. "Now where is Alan's wife?" she asked.

Wendy answered. "Lillian had to return some props, so she'll be a few minutes late."

The rehearsal began. There were only a few pages in the folder I had been given. At the top of the first one was the name of my character and a brief description: "Seton Cram mid-forties, rich, stockbroker." I quickly figured out that the few words on the line above my speeches must be my cue, so I listened intently. I finally heard words that matched and then I spoke.

"No, not yet, Alan," Miss Forbes interrupted, "you're not in this scene."

Everyone looked at me. At that moment, a woman came rushing down the aisle. She was a tough, bleached blond in her fifties with a heavily lined face and a lit cigarette clamped between her teeth. "I'm so sorry to be late, Marla," she said.

"That's all right, darling," Miss Forbes replied. "Wendy told us you would be. Alan," she made a sweeping gesture, "this is your wife. Lillian, this is Alan."

The rehearsal only lasted two hours. All the actors were tired from opening night. They just mumbled their lines. Miss Forbes, who was directing, never looked up from the Samuel French paper copy of

Phillip Barry's *Holiday* that she held in her hand. She seemed to be reading the directions she gave from the book. Everyone had sides like mine, but the leads had many more pages than I did.

"Cross over to the sofa, Trilby, and sit down," Miss Forbes sang out from her position on the audience side of the footlights. Trilby obeyed, saying her line without any inflection as she wrote the move down. I did the same when it came to my scene. "Walk to the window and look out as you say that, Alan," Miss Forbes would command and I, mumbling like the others, stopped being afraid.

I felt very awkward when I stood next to Lillian. I knew we must make a ridiculous couple. I had had a lot of trouble trying to brush my hair down that day and it was sticking straight up on one side. I wished I had worn something better than my second-best slack suit, but Lillian was in shorts and a blouse covered in strings of beads, so I guessed it was all right. I noticed all the veins in her legs, but we would be in evening clothes in the play so the audience wouldn't see them.

When we were dismissed, Miss Forbes called out to me as I was leaving. "Alan."

"Yes, Miss Forbes?" I was sure I was about to be fired.

"I've told you to call me Marla," she said. "I never want to hear Miss Forbes again! Now, you're not free yet. I have to drive you into Gloucester to rent you a tuxedo."

As the week went on, I became more confident. Everyone was encouraging except leading man Rusty. That was okay with me because I couldn't stand him anyway. Flo, the little character lady, took me under her wing so I finally had a friend. I only saw the other actors at rehearsals since they were still doing the French farce in the evening. I usually went swimming at the town beach in the late afternoon and had dinner with Mother at one of the many restaurants in the evening. She showed up at the theater one day and insisted on meeting the cast. They were all charming to her.

Afterward, she said she liked Rusty the best. I didn't say anything.

Chapter 29

Opening night, I borrowed some makeup from Jack, the character man. He must have sensed my fear, because he tried hard to buoy me up. He kidded me as I covered my face with a base and then drew age lines around my eyes with an eyebrow pencil. He told me to shadow under my eyes and rub some white into my temples and sideburns. He then made a few corrections and set it all with a dusting of powder. I looked rather ill but no longer sixteen.

Lillian had put up her hair and was wearing her idea of society clothes a gold and navy-blue striped blouse over a black full skirt. As we stood waiting for our entrance, I noticed my tuxedo pants had been shortened and I had forgotten to change my blue socks. For a moment I panicked and thought I'd quickly run back to the dressing room and change them. Instead, Lillian took my arm and said, "There's the cue. Break a leg."

I remembered all my lines and all the movements Marla had given to me in rehearsal. She hadn't said anything about the character, so I'd invented one myself. I could feel that I had a tense smile on my face, but I couldn't relax enough to get rid of it. I did get a chance to look out front. There was a small group of people huddled near the stage. They weren't making a sound. Flo had told me that *Holiday* was "high comedy." That meant that there weren't any laughs, but still the people seemed strangely silent.

When I walked over to get the cigarette box to offer Lillian one, I noticed that a flat in the back wall had been put in upside down, so it didn't match the others. I thought I'd better tell Wendy to fix it. Suddenly I realized that I'd heard my cue and my stomach plunged. I said my line, but I'd been a million miles away. I had almost caused a disaster.

There was a smattering of applause at the final curtain. Marla came backstage gushing with praise as if we'd had a smash hit. She came over to me. "You were very good," she said. "Now, be here at eleven in the morning. I have a marvelous role for you in the new play."

My mother didn't like *Holiday*. She didn't think much of Trilby, who played the lead, but she praised me. There was to be a party at the actors' house, but Mother thought I should get some sleep. When we returned to the room she said as she undressed, "There was someone in back of me who said something about the performance that I thought was very good. I wrote it down." She opened her pocketbook and took out an envelope that she unfolded. She read from the back of it. "You can't make a silk purse out of a sow's ear." I wasn't quite sure what that had to do with the play, but I nodded and went to bed.

When I arrived at the theater the next morning, I was amazed to discover so many people. Flo had told me that six actors were being brought up from New York for the play that was to be tried out to see if it was good enough for Broadway. *What luck*, I thought. *If it goes to New York and I'm in it, all my problems will be solved.* As the Rockport actors arrived, there were shouts and screams from the New York actors. They all seemed to know each other, and I felt totally left out. Flo told me Rusty was playing the lead. He acted more important than ever and ignored me, as usual.

Marla arrived with her dog, a scarf around her head, and the same rumpled slack suit she'd had on the night before. "Darlings," she called everyone to order. "I want you to meet the two boys who've written the most wonderful play." She indicated two men in their thirties, and everyone shook their hands. Wendy appeared and handed out sides to the actors.

I took mine over to the back of the auditorium and sat down. Printed on the blue cover was *Ah Theater*. Inside, on the first page, was my character "Horace Willoughby." After it was printed "a young man who is a neurasthenic." I had no idea what that meant, and I certainly wasn't going to ask anyone. If I could get through the rehearsal, I'd go to the library and look it up.

The reading began and I discovered that Marla was playing the female lead as well as directing. It was obvious the play had been written for her since the character was a director and a nightclub singer. Rusty was to play a young actor who pretended to be in love with her so he could get the lead in the play. When they got to a scene in which Marla was to sit at a piano and sing to Rusty, Marla put down her script.

"I want you to hear the song I've written to sing in the play, " she said. She walked over to an upright piano that was pushed against the back wall. We all followed her and stood around as she played and sang in her deep, throaty voice:

"I thought that love was a bore,
Those nights with men were a chore.
To listen to their endless schemes
Put an end to all my dreams,
But then you came my way
And how I wanted you to stay.
Love became a wonderful game
That only we two could play."

As Marla played a few chords on the piano to back up her last note, the company burst into applause. I felt I was part of a sophisticated New York show that was going to be a big hit. I envied Rusty for playing the role I felt I should have had. *Maybe he'll get sick, I thought, and they'll ask me to replace him.* I listened for my first cue. I gathered, from what the other characters said about me, that in the play I was a young actor who was just beginning and so nervous he could barely speak. He kept repeating to himself, "Every day, in every way, I'm getting better and better."

The cast laughed as I read my lines. I didn't know what they were laughing at, but it made me feel good. When we got to the third act, I had a big scene where everyone tried to get me to go onstage to say my one line. When it came time for me to speak, I blurted out nervously, "People are people and there's nothing you can do about it!" Everyone applauded and I felt much more a part of the group than I had at the beginning of the rehearsal.

Mother told me at dinner that she was going home. We were eating fried clams at a candlelit seafood restaurant on Bear Skin Neck. "I really should get home to Daddy," she said. "I think all of the people in the company are nice and that you'll be perfectly safe."

I tried not to show how overjoyed I was. "I hate for you to leave," I said, "but I know there's nothing for you to do here."

"I'm confident that you can take care of yourself," she replied, "but I don't want you living alone in case you get sick. I've spoken to Rusty and he's going to move in with you."

I was stunned. "I don't like Rusty."

"He's the nicest one of all of them. He'll be a good influence on you."

"Can't I just live in the actor's house? I wouldn't be alone."

"I'll feel better if you just stay where you are. I've already settled it with Rusty, unless you'd rather I stayed."

"You know I'd like you to stay, but I know you have to get back. I'll room with Rusty."

After I took Mother to the bus the next day, I went back to the rooming house. I discovered several suitcases sitting on the floor next to my bed. It was as if someone foreign had invaded my territory and I felt uneasy.

I had seen Rusty at the rehearsal, but he'd said nothing about moving in with me. Then after the performance, he came over to me. "I'll walk to the room with you," he said. As we went down the hill, he kept up a steady stream of talk about New York, making the rounds of the agents' offices, casting calls, and new plays he was up for. He seemed to know everyone who was important. I told him how little I knew about being an actor and getting work. "Don't worry," he said, "if you go to New York, I'll help you out." I was amazed. He'd never even said "hello" to me before.

When we got to the room, I helped him unpack. There were dozens of shirts and slacks in bright colors, and cashmere sweaters, as well as suits and sport jackets. I pushed my few things way to the side of the closet to make room for him.

He went first to the bathroom at the end of the hall. Then I went, and when I returned, after brushing my teeth, I started to get into my bed. He was lying down in his shorts.

"No," he said. "Let's talk for a while. Come over here so we don't make too much noise," he smoothed a place by his leg.

I didn't want to be rude, so I sat there gingerly. I was suddenly afraid he was going to touch me, and I didn't know how to respond. Fortunately, nothing happened. After a moment he said, "Look, it's going to be a long summer and we're going to need sex. We might as well have it together."

I was amazed. It was so impersonal. As if he had settled it all by himself. I'd always thought that sex came out of loving. That was the way it was with Roger. "I hate to say it," I said awkwardly, "and I think you're very handsome, Rusty, but I just don't feel anything."

Rusty laughed. "Don't be ridiculous," he said, "I don't feel anything either. It's just a question of getting your rocks off." He pulled back the covers. "Now get into bed or we'll never get to sleep."

I didn't know what to do. I wished Roger were there to help me deal with it. I still hadn't heard a word from him. Flo worked in the box office and I had alerted her to watch out for a letter for me, but so far nothing had arrived. I'd been rationalizing that not enough time had gone by for him to get my letter from Brookline and send me one back. Any day, I knew I'd hear. I stood up and walked over to my own bed. I didn't know what to say without making Rusty angry. But I hadn't counted on Rusty's egomania.

"Okay," Rusty said. "I'm tired, too. There'll be plenty of other nights."

When I awoke the next morning, he was standing in front of the mirror sprinkling his thick hair with Vitalis. He combed it lovingly and set a wave in the front with the flat of his hand. As I watched him, I formulated a plan. Later that day, I went to the actors' house and found a tiny room off the kitchen that was unused since it had no door. There were no other rooms available, but I could put a blanket over the doorway. I went to see Flo and told her I wanted to save some money and move into the tiny room. She said she'd get a small bed moved in there and give me some paint to freshen it up. She also told me no letter had come.

That night I waited in the room for Rusty, who had gone to have drinks with friends. When he came in and saw me sitting up in bed, he said, "Hello," and closed the door.

I took a deep breath to get my courage. "Rusty," I said, "I'm moving out. I won't do it until the end of the week so nobody will think there's anything funny. I don't want anything more to do with you."

He didn't even turn around as he took off his shirt. "Suit yourself," he said.

Chapter 30

I woke up in the actors' house to what sounded like a refrigerator. For a minute I didn't know where I was. Then I remembered and smiled. I loved my little room next to the kitchen. I felt so safe. I spent my time after rehearsals painting it white, two coats, and it was sparkling clean. A piece of cheesecloth was nailed over the doorway until I could find a blanket. It didn't keep out the noise or the light, but it gave the illusion of privacy. I could see Trilby through it now, feeding her baby. Everyone had been so welcoming. I felt a part of a real family for the first time in my life. Then I had a sudden sense of dread. I remembered tonight was the opening of the play. I forced myself to get up.

The dress rehearsal went badly, but Flo told me that was traditional in the theater. It meant that the opening would be a smash. I didn't see how it would be, in just a few hours, with so many things going wrong. Marla asked me to ride to Gloucester with her, and I was glad not to be alone. I had started to get a case of the jitters and every once in a while, I began to shake as if I had a severe chill.

On the drive, Marla told me that in addition to the people coming up from New York, there were fifty reservations, the most they'd ever had. It made me feel even worse. Then Marla took a piece of paper from behind her back that she seemed to have been hiding. "Here's your surprise, Alan," she said. She handed me a program with *Ah Theater* at the top and a list of the actors and their roles. I quickly skimmed down and there was my name, but now it was spelled Shayne instead of Schein. A few days before, Marla had convinced me that no one would be able to say my name correctly with the real spelling. "They'll say 'Shine' or 'Scean,'" she said. Part of me was hesitant as I wondered if she wanted me to change it because it sounded Jewish, but she told me "Shayne" was a perfect name for a star. When my father had a photography studio, it was called "The Shayne Studio," so I figured if the family found out, they couldn't very well say anything about it.

I had saved four dollars in rent by moving into the actors' house, so I used it to buy some makeup. I managed to get through the day, but all I could think of was that in a short time, I would be standing on the stage in front of all those people. As the moment drew nearer, my fear increased. At dinner with the other actors, I couldn't manage anything but soda water. No one let on to me that they knew I was terrified. They just kept encouraging me.

The curtain went up promptly at eight-thirty so that the Gloucester critic could file her review in time. I managed to get through the first act, but I was so nervous, I didn't wait for my laughs. I talked right through them. In the intermission, Marla and the authors sought me out to tell me how good I was. All I could think of was that they only said it to give me the courage to get through the rest of the play. It made me feel worse.

In the second act, all I had to do was wear a gypsy costume and help carry a bathtub on stage. That went all right. But the third act was where I had the most to do. It was all about everyone trying to get my character, who had stage fright, to go on stage and deliver the final line of the play. I was so scared that I didn't have to act, and the audience laughed hysterically. When I managed to deliver my one line, "People are people and there's nothing you can do about it," the audience screamed, and the curtain came down to wild applause.

After the curtain call, I climbed the stairs to the dressing room that the men shared. No one said anything to me as I took off my costume and started to remove my makeup. They all talked to each other about how much work the play needed and how lucky they were to have gotten through it. I felt depressed. I must have overacted. I had felt so real in my nervousness, but it may have been too much.

I heard Flo call from outside the door, "Everybody decent?" When all the men chorused, "Yes," she came in and walked over to me. "The critic of the Gloucester paper wants to interview you," she said. "She's waiting in Marla's office."

I jumped up and ran to the door. When I got to the stairs, I realized I was in my underwear and my face was covered with cold cream.

The critic turned out to be a motherly woman in her forties. It was my first interview and I didn't quite know how to behave. I wondered if I should try to act as if it happened all the time, but I couldn't lie when she asked my age.

"You're a beginner!" she said. "I'm amazed. You haven't had any training?" I told her everything that had happened to me so far and she clucked like a hen. "I know you're going to have a wonderful career."

All the actors congratulated me and insisted I come to the party at the house. Everyone proceeded to get a little drunk and they even let me have one glass of wine. They raked the play, and their performances, over the coals. But they did nothing but praise me and make me feel wanted. Rusty didn't mix with the actors, so he wasn't there to spoil the evening.

At one point, Marla began to sing a song with risque lyrics that made everyone laugh:

"A seedy motel on the edge of town,
An old desk clerk with a perpetual frown,
A squeaky mattress and a woman's moan
The constant ring of an unanswered phone.
We didn't bother to even undress,
All we wanted was to cure our stress.
When it was done, we said goodbye
Returning to our spouses with the usual lie."

I sat on the floor, leaning against the seat of a chair and sipping my wine. This is the most wonderful life, I thought. A critic said I was good and I'm a part of a family.

Marla tapped on her glass to get everyone's attention. When it was quiet, she said, "I'm sad to tell you that I'm closing the theater."

Chapter 31

Marla had scheduled the new play to run for two weeks, so we struggled on until the last performance, with only a few people in attendance. Mother and Dad came to pick me up. I had said goodbye to everyone, and it felt like the end of the world. Flo had to stay at the theater for several weeks to wind things up, so she said she would look out for the letter I was still expecting. It was now so many weeks since I had written to Roger and still no answer. I began to worry that something had happened to him. Could he have been sent overseas so soon? I didn't know anyone who could give me any information. I couldn't contact his mother; I didn't even know how to reach her.

I wrote a long letter to Roger when I got back to Brookline describing my time at the theater. I tried to make it funny, so he'd be amused. Maybe, he had never gotten any of the letters I sent. I hoped at least he would get this one.

After Labor Day, I read in the paper that the Tributary Theater in Boston was holding open auditions for *Much Ado About Nothing*. I memorized a Shakespeare monologue and went into town and, after waiting hours for my turn, stood on the bare stage that was almost dark. I didn't think they could see me, so I spoke up. In a way, it was helpful that I couldn't see them, so I wasn't scared. I began, "Oh that this too, too solid flesh would melt" from *Hamlet*. I kept thinking they would stop me, but I got all the way to the end. I expected, "Don't call us, we'll call you" but they gave me a role on the spot. We rehearsed nights for several weeks and opened to very good notices. Mine read, "A well-spoken, handsome Claudio."

One of the actors in the play told me that since so many young men were being drafted from the radio stations, I might have a chance to get a job as an announcer. I did have a very deep voice for my age, and I was ready to try anything to find work. Hanging around the house was making me depressed. I began to audition whenever anyone would let me, but so far all I had gotten was "We'll call you if there's an opening."

In early November, as the leaves were swirling in the wind that came off the Charles River, I climbed a tall flight of stairs to a small reception room with cheap plastic and chrome furniture. There was a store-sized window through which I could see an announcer talking into a microphone. As I stood waiting for someone to appear, a tall, almost obese man in a blue suit came through a door and looked at me. "Are you being helped?" he asked in a bass voice.

"I'd like to see someone about an audition," I said shyly.

"What about me?" the fat man broke into a wide smile. His attitude was so jovial that I relaxed completely. He introduced himself as John Kiley and said he was the head of the radio station.

He took me into an empty studio where he gave me some papers to read and then he went into a control room to listen. I sat at a table in front of a microphone and read what he'd given me. I waited to hear his voice tell me to stop, but instead I kept hearing, "Go on, go on." I read commercials, news, and even introductions to musical pieces. I didn't feel at all nervous. I just spoke into the mike as if I were talking to someone I knew. I heard the door open and Mr. Kiley walked over to me. His face was wreathed in smiles.

"You're very good," he said. "I think one of the guys is about to be drafted, and I'd like to give you a try."

"Do you mean soon?" I asked. I didn't dare believe that my work problems could actually be solved so easily.

"Let me make a call or two," the fat man said, "and I'll let you know tonight."

I started the job the following week. As I was about to go on the air for the first time, Mr. Kiley stood by my side. "Alan, you're about to be heard by over a million people." Strangely enough, I didn't get ruffled at all. If anything, it made me excited. I felt the blood pumping through me and giving me a rush. When I finished, Mr. Kiley clapped me on the back and said, "Alan, you're a born announcer!"

Radio announcing turned out to be anything but glamorous. I was alone in an insulated ten-foot square space for most of my eight-hour day. I read the news, played records and talked. I discovered that I could talk endlessly on almost any subject, so long as I didn't need too many facts. This ability stood me in good stead for filling minutes of airtime when the scripts were too short. Every fifteen or thirty minutes, I alternated programs with Dick Purcell, a small, undistinguished man in his early forties. His only vanity seemed to be a luxuriant head of hair that he was constantly combing. He was very bright and amusing. Dick was a shot of fresh air in the solitary life I now lived. I worked from early in the morning to late afternoon, seeing only the engineer through the huge window and then Dick when he came to take over from me.

A month went by without any routine change. I took the subway to work every day, read whatever was handed to me, and spun records. All my friends were at school, so I spent my free time at home. My parents' arguments intensified. Somehow, my success as a radio announcer had become a catalyst that caused recriminations between by mother and my father. She accused him of not making enough money to let them live properly. He retaliated with the complaint that she was always playing cards and not taking care of the apartment. My brother was at school, so I became the scapegoat.

One night, Mr. Kiley had gotten me a job to introduce speakers at a banquet he was going to. I would be paid twenty-five dollars. He said he'd be by to pick me up at seven. I was very excited and a little nervous as I sat at the kitchen table with my parents. I picked at my food and kept looking at my watch.

"Finish your dinner," my father said.

"I'm just not hungry."

"You eat everything on your plate or you're not going out."

"I'm just too excited to eat," I explained, "and Mr. Kiley will be here any minute."

"I told you, you're not going anywhere unless you eat that food."

I was upset and suddenly stubborn. "I don't have to. I'm going to go to work and I'm going to make twenty-five dollars. I don't have to eat anything more."

My father got up from his chair, walked over to me, and slapped me hard in the face. I ran to my room where I slammed the door. I sat waiting, trying to calm down. When the doorbell rang, I took my coat and went out without seeing my parents.

I had to find a way to get away from them.

Chapter 32

Once a week, the radio station broadcast a live mystery program featuring actors appearing in Boston plays. The show was late at night, long after I finished work, but I always tried to listen to it. I had recently been assigned an interview program where I spoke with some of the same actors, so listening helped me to talk about their performances when I met them. It immediately broke the ice. I had heard a particularly gruesome thriller entitled *The Fog Drips Blood* starring Guerita Donnelly, who was playing a small role in a touring company of the Broadway hit *Junior Miss*. I laughed as she used her husky, British-accented voice to wring every bit of melodrama out of the amateurish script.

The next morning, I was alone in the studio playing records, with only the engineer behind the glass partition to keep me company. I sipped my stale coffee and occasionally answered the phone if anyone called with a request. The air conditioner was barely adequate, and the room smelled of old cigarettes. At the end of the day, I always had a slight headache from the lack of oxygen.

The phone lit up and I finished my introduction, put the needle on the record, and signaled the engineer to bring up the volume. I then picked up the phone. A smoky, slightly drunken voice said, "This is the fog drips blood."

"Good morning, Miss Donnelly," I said without the slightest hesitation. There was no mistaking the voice I had heard the night before. She was delighted that I knew who she was, and we began to talk. She confessed she was lonely and the only people she knew in Boston were at the radio station. I sensed that she was hung over and tried to cheer her up. I told her to turn on her radio to 830 and then I dedicated records to her. "This one is for a lovely lady in bed," I said into the microphone. When I went back to talk to her, she was laughing gleefully. I went about my work and rather enjoyed the distraction. Suddenly, she said she was coming to the station that afternoon to be interviewed. I told her it must be my program.

"You see," she said seductively, "you can't get away from me."

The interview went very well. Gerry, as she insisted that I call her, turned out to be a dumpy, middle-aged woman with smeared makeup and rumpled clothes, but with the speaking voice of a Duchess. However, the words she spoke sounded as if they were trying to walk a straight line for a sobriety test. With her was Louis Beachner, a handsome young actor several years older than I, who played the juvenile lead in the play.

The three of us chatted amiably and I asked all my usual questions about their careers. When I offered them coffee afterward, we sat down and they began to question me. I confessed that I wanted to be an actor and was planning to go to New York as soon as I could save enough money.

"Don't," said Gerry imperiously. "It could be five years before you get a role in a play on Broadway."

When it was time for them to leave, they invited me to their show. I said I would be free the following night.

"We'll leave a ticket in your name at the box office," Louis said. I noticed that he had the slightest British accent too, though he'd said in the interview that he was from Jersey City.

I felt like royalty as I sat in an aisle seat in the orchestra. I had never been able to afford anything more than the fifty-five cents it cost to get a ticket in the second balcony. I watched the comedy about a young precocious girl turning into a beautiful young woman. All I could concentrate on were the roles I could possibly have played. I constantly searched the plays that came to Boston for parts I thought I could have gotten if I had only been in New York. There were at least three boyfriends for the girl's older sister that I thought I could play. There was only one role, of a jock football player who was brutish and disgusting, that was not a possibility. I squirmed when the actor yelled and bounded about the stage.

After the show, I went backstage to see Gerry and Louis. She had been superb as a tough, wisecracking maid, and he had been appropriately handsome and charming as the boy who takes out the girl when she has turned into a beautiful young woman. Over sandwiches at a delicatessen, I spoke again of my dream to go to New York and be an actor. They were both sympathetic but told me I would be crazy to try New York until I had enough money to support myself while I waited for something to happen.

"Remember what I told you at the radio station," Gerry said. "It could be five years before you ever get a play on Broadway."

A week later, Gerry called the radio station. When she got me on the phone she said, "You won't believe this, but one of the boys in the show has been drafted and you're going to get the role."

I was flabbergasted. "What are you talking about?"

"I've already spoken to the stage manager," she said, "and you're going to get a reading and, no question, you'll get the part."

For a moment I thought it might be possible, but I didn't dare believe it. "Which part is it?" I asked as I held my breath.

"The football player," Gerry said. "It's the best part of any of the boys."

My heart sank. For a moment I'd gotten away from my family, and finally, I had become an actor. Now the fantasy was shattered. I had a mound of brown hair and a thin face and body that was more suitable for playing a poet. No one would ever believe me as a loutish football player. "Thanks," I said crestfallen, "but I don't think I could be right for that."

"What's the matter with you?" Gerry said. "You want to be an actor, don't you? I'm going to coach you, so you have nothing to worry about. We'll get you into the show tonight and you can study the scene. Come on. Cheer up. You're going to get it!"

I sat in the theater watching the play again. My spine tingled with fear when it came time for the football player to enter. With a great roar, the actor came on and went barreling down on the girl's father, who had a New Year's Day hangover. He slapped the older man hard on the back and then proceeded to imitate going bowling with loud noises, exacerbating the man's headache. The most unbearable moment came when he took a piece of candy out of a bowl, tasted it, said "cream" with disgust and wiped what was left on his spanking clean, camel hair overcoat. The audience loved it, but I was revolted.

Later, I told Gerry and Louis, "I just don't see how I can do this role."

"You said you wanted to go to New York," Gerry replied. "Well, here's a God-given opportunity to get you there." She handed me a couple of half-pages stapled between cardboard covers. "Here are the sides. Just learn them and I'll rehearse you. You're going to be fine."

I was in a daze of fear the day of the audition. I had memorized the lines and rehearsed over and over. Gerry had been ill and unable to help me, but I had gone back to the play several times. I knew every move and gesture the actor made. I couldn't find anything in myself that was like the role, so I decided to just try and copy what I saw. I felt grotesque and just longed for it all to be over. I wished I could get out of the reading, but I couldn't be ungrateful to Gerry and Louis.

When I arrived at the theater before the show, the old doorman had a message for me. "Miss Donnelly wants to see you in her dressing room before you audition."

I found Gerry waiting for me. She held out the camel hair coat and a bright yellow scarf that the football player wore in the play.

"I stole these from the wardrobe room," she said mischievously. "Put them on."

I put on the coat that was much too big for me and she wrapped the scarf around my neck. I could see in the makeup mirror that I looked like a poster to raise money for needy children.

"You look perfect," Gerry said, "but let's just roll up the sleeves."

She took my arm and guided me out onto the stage. The curtain was up since it wasn't time to let in the audience. A big bulb in a wire cage hung from the ceiling. It cast a murky light through which

I could barely make out a little man in the wings who looked like an old leprechaun.

"What do you think, Bill?" Gerry had raised her voice. "Doesn't he look the part?"

The man looked me up and down, squinting his eyes in the semi-darkness. He didn't seem to recognize that I was wearing the costume from the show. "Yuh," he said, "he could be right. Certainly, save money from bringing someone up from New York if he can do it. Let's hear him." He walked out to the stairs that would take him to the front of the house.

Gerry took the moment to whisper to me. "Yell really loud. He's a little hard of hearing." She rushed out after him.

I noticed that the stage manager staggered, and I wondered if he were drunk, but I couldn't think about it now. I had to pull myself together and get through this ordeal. When I heard a voice yell, "All right, go ahead," I opened the door onto the set and charged in as if I'd been shot out of a cannon. I shouted the lines as loud as I could and mimicked the actor I had studied. No one was reading my cues, so I just kept going like a whirlwind. When I finished, I stood panting and perspiring in the heavy coat. There wasn't a sound from the front until the little man came to the footlights and looked up at me. "Not bad," he said pursing his lips. "You could do with some rehearsal."

"He was great," Gerry hollered from her seat.

The stage manager gave her a disapproving look and then turned to me. "You open in Hartford on Christmas Day."

Chapter 33

I walked into the kitchen where my parents were listening to the war news on the radio. I had a trump card since I was to receive the actor's minimum salary for a road show fifty-five dollars a week. It was five dollars more than my father was making in his new job as an insurance instructor. He had finally given up photography after years of struggling.

When I made them turn down the radio and listen to my good fortune and the money I would make, my father hit the ceiling. "Absolutely not! Under no circumstances."

My mother agreed and the arguments began. "You're only seventeen," my mother began. "You should be going to college."

"You have a good job as a radio announcer," my father overrode her. "There's a great future in radio. And the people are not awful the way they are in the theater."

I fought for my life. "I'll never forgive you if I lose this opportunity. I could never buy this kind of experience and they're paying me a fortune to do it." I dragged out all the reasons that I'd used to get them to let me go to summer stock, but they fell on deaf ears. This time my parents would not give in. I didn't know what to do. Because of my age, one parent had to sign the contract so I couldn't just run away. The stage manager had given me a one-way ticket to Hartford, but it wouldn't do me any good without a signed contract. I didn't tell Gerry or Louis about my parents' refusal. I was afraid they'd tell someone in the company, and I'd be replaced.

The days that followed were agony. I told my boss Mr. Kiley at the station and he was very supportive. He said he wouldn't hire anyone else in the event that I couldn't change my parents' minds, but he hoped I'd be able to go. I swallowed my pride and asked my brother to help me but of course he wouldn't. I wasn't surprised. I called my rich aunt and uncle and they were as opposed to me being an actor as my parents were.

The company had the week before Christmas off, but I went to see the play once more before closing night in Boston. I still found my role totally foreign. I had been reading Stanislavsky's *An Actor Prepares*. He seemed to say that you had to find some quality in the character you were playing that was similar to something in you. I still hadn't found it yet, but I was sure I would if I could just get to Hartford.

I went backstage to see Gerry and Louis. They told me that Gerry was leaving the play to have a minor operation. That was a blow since I'd counted on her to coach me as she had promised. She said Louis would help me. He suggested we share a room at the hotel in Hartford in case I needed help with my lines. I said that would be great, and I thought it would save money as well. As we said goodbye, I thought of telling them that I might not be in the play at all. But I still held out hope that it would happen.

I had not heard from Roger in almost eight months. My letters to the Officers Training School had not been returned, so I assumed he was still there. I wanted to tell someone what I was going through, and Roger was the only one who had ever taken any interest in me. I decided to write him one last time. I told him that I had to get away from my parents. He knew my father had always been cold and distant. I wrote that I loved my mother fiercely when I was a child, but she had changed. Or maybe I had changed. She now only thought of her card games and her women's club meetings. I thought it might make Roger laugh, so I wrote that she had just been appointed the head of entertainment for the past presidents' dinner at her club. She was spending her days writing lyrics to honor the women using songs the members could sing. She went around the house singing as she wrote: to the tune of "I Love You Truly," "Dora Wyzanski, we all love you;" and to the middle section of "Bei Mir Bist Du Schoen," "Sadie Margolis always lends a helping hand." There were twenty past presidents, so she was very busy. Despite my worry about the play, I couldn't help laughing at each song I heard.

In the midst of the turmoil, my mother started to burden me with confessions about how strained her relationship with my father had become. One day she said, "Your father is not a sexual man." I didn't remind her that she had had two sons with him. She went on to tell me that she really loved her childhood sweetheart in Kansas and had heard that his wife died. She said she'd be hearing from him any day. I was pretty sure it was all in her imagination.

I wrote Roger of my history of wanting to be an actor, from the day I met him on the beach and said it out loud for the first time. I went through Rockport, acting in Shakespeare, and now the radio announcing. I knew Roger couldn't help me but writing him was as if I were talking to him again. I got everything off my chest and determined, somehow, that I would open in the play on Christmas Day. I ended the letter with: "If you're ever in a city where *Junior Miss* is playing, find out if I'm in the cast."

As the time drew near for me to leave for Hartford, I redoubled my efforts to make my parents change their minds. They were immovable. No matter what my argument was, they refuted it, and no threat I made was taken seriously. I had about given up when the most amazing thing happened. I became very ill. I coughed, I sneezed, I ran a fever, and I went to bed. It was the one idea that never would have occurred to me and yet, it was infallible. My father related better to illness than to anything else. When he saw that I had made myself sick at the prospect of not acting in the play, he couldn't continue his opposition. All of his admonitions about being careful to eat right, sleep right, dress warmly, not to do too much exercise were worthless if I was going to be an invalid through mental anguish.

On Christmas morning, I got out of bed, dressed, packed my bag, and put the contract in front of my father. He signed it. He didn't, however, give me verbal permission to go. I didn't need it. My parents drove me to the Back Bay Station. I got on the train with a temperature of a hundred and one and a bad case of laryngitis. I was on my way to Hartford and my debut as a professional actor.

Chapter 34

I slept most of the way on the train and when I woke, I had flashbacks of my mother begging me for the last time not to go and my father warning me to get plenty of sleep and not to smoke. The cold, gray light of the New England winter chilled me as it came through the window of the train, but I could still feel sweat running down my back from the fever. I felt as if I were going to prison, not to the beginning of my great stage career. I kept taking the sides out of my pocket and going over my lines. I had known them perfectly for a week but now I kept forgetting them, in a different place every time. I felt detached. It was all happening to someone else, not me. If only they had rehearsed me in Boston. The stage manager said he was too busy, and that there was time enough to do it before the show in Hartford. My heart began to race. I tried to tell myself that it was because of my cold. A voice inside me kept saying, "You're scared out of your wits." I knew it was true.

Arriving at the Bond Annex Hotel where Louis had reserved a room for us was easy. I seemed to be floating and wasn't aware of hailing a cab or the weight of my two suitcases. I was sailing in the air on a beautiful balloon that landed in a room with two beds. Louis was already there. He helped me with my bags and told me what he'd done on his week off in New York. Once in a while, I heard something through the fog of my clogged ears. I made out that at two o'clock, he would walk me over to the theater for a rehearsal. They'd given him the message when they couldn't reach me.

My nose began to bleed on the way to the theater. I said to Louis, "What'll I do if it starts to bleed in the middle of the scene?"

"That would never happen," Louis assured me. I wondered how he could know.

There was already a telegram from my parents waiting for me at the theater "Hope you feel well and made good." I guess they thought it would arrive later. If only it were all over. Louis left me alone and I wandered out onto the stage. It was immense. The set for the play only took up a small section. The rest was shrouded in darkness and looked like pictures I'd seen of the catacombs in Rome. I walked to the footlights and looked at the empty auditorium that seemed to stretch into infinity. The orchestra pit was as big as an Olympic-sized swimming pool. "My God," I thought, "the audience will never hear me."

My nose was so stuffed and my ears so blocked that I barely made out the stage manager who called as he approached, "Let's get started. I only have a few minutes."

"Are the other actors coming?" I asked.

"Of course," he said. "Just walk through it for me until they arrive."

I started to run through the scene. I came roaring in the door and slapped an imaginary actor on the back. "Happy New Year," I yelled. "We're going bowling." I went on screaming and then did my imitation of throwing the ball and watching it make a strike at the back of the theater.

"No, no, no," shouted the stage manager, "that doesn't look like you're bowling. It looks like you're giving somebody a triple goose." He walked up on stage. If only I hadn't been sick, I could have gone bowling and learned how. I'd never bowled in my life. A lone light bulb hung down, casting a pall on the two of us. We looked like the only people left in a bombed-out world.

"Look," the older man said. "Here's how you do it."

I watched him hold his fingers in an arthritic, clutching gesture as he threw an imaginary ball at the empty playhouse. I tried desperately to copy the gnarled, twisted hand. Since he made no further comment, I thought I must be doing it right. Much later I discovered that he was missing one finger so what I was copying was unrecognizable to anyone who'd ever bowled.

The actors arrived. I had met them in Boston, and they were

friendly and welcoming. We started to rehearse the scene. I forgot my lines after my second speech, and I couldn't go on. My nose started to bleed so the stage manager waited until it stopped. When we began again, I forgot my lines in a different place. The stage manager came running up on the stage, yelling furiously.

"I can't hear a word you're saying, and you don't know your lines," he said.

I felt terribly embarrassed in front of the others. "I have a cold and I took a lot of aspirin."

"Well, let's try it again," the little man snapped. "If you don't know your lines, the understudy can go on and you can play the part in Philadelphia."

I thought I'd been given a reprieve until one of the actors whispered, "If you don't go on tonight, you'll never go on." I did a little better in the next rehearsal but still went blank in the middle of the scene.

"All right," the stage manager called out, "that's enough for now." As everyone started to leave, he came over to me. "Listen," he said, "you'd better study all afternoon. I'll go over your lines with you before the show. If you're not word perfect, you don't go on."

Louis cued me in the scene all afternoon. I felt guilty taking so much of his time, but he said he and Gerry had gotten me into all this, and he was determined to help me make it a success. From time to time, I fell asleep. I would wake with a start, feeling groggy, and ask Louis to go over my lines with me again.

Before the curtain, the stage manager listened to me recite the words. I remembered them all. "Please let me go on," I begged.

"All right," the older man agreed. "I've got my fingers crossed."

I sat in my dressing room and put on my makeup. Louis had given me a beautiful makeup kit that he said was a Christmas present from him and Gerry. With all I'd had on my mind, it hadn't occurred to me to buy something for Louis. I felt embarrassed, but Louis assured me that it was also an opening night gift that was theater tradition, so

I felt better. The actor sharing my dressing room said, "I hear we're almost full and the place seats thirty-five hundred."

I felt like I was in a dream where walls separated me from the rest of the world. I put on the camel hair coat. The sleeves were shortened, but I could see in the mirror that I still looked ridiculous in it. I went down to the stage and waited in the wings for my cue. All I could think of was whether my nose would start to bleed again. As it got close to the moment for my entrance, I walked into position behind the door of the set. I kept going over and over my lines, desperately, saying them faster and faster as the time got closer. Then I heard the doorbell that was rung by the stage manager who did all the sound effects. I took a deep breath as the girl's footsteps reverberated as she came closer to the other side of the door. And then it opened.

"Happy New Year, Lois, old girl, old girl," I yelled.

I felt my arm taken as I was guided toward the footlights. I was aware of a great black pit with thousands of heads looking at me.

"This is my father," Lois said.

I whacked him on the back, yelling all the while, "Happy New Year, Happy New Year!"

There was a tremendous laugh as the actor playing the father almost fell over from the slap and made a grimace of agony from his hangover. The roar from the audience seemed to awaken me and I became a dynamo, yelling every line and getting enormous guffaws. When I grabbed Lois and sailed out the door, slamming it hard, I heard the audience applaud. The actors who had been watching the scene from the wings ran over to congratulate me.

"The boy who had your part never got a hand," the girl who played Lois said.

I felt something was wrong. I went over to the stage manager. He looked at me for a moment, and then said, "It was okay."

"Can we rehearse tomorrow?" I asked.

"What do you mean?" the wizened face looked surprised. "It's a matinee day. And what's the difference. You got a hand, didn't you?" He turned away.

I went back to the others feeling that something was not right. Maybe the audience applauded because I had made such a fool of myself. But the cast acted as if I'd had a triumph.

Chapter 35

Several weeks later, when we were playing in Philadelphia, I arrived at the theater to get ready for the evening performance. I found a letter in my mailbox. My first thought was that my mother had forwarded it and finally, I was hearing from Roger. I opened it and saw it was from the producers of *Junior Miss*. It was typewritten and only consisted of three lines:

In accordance with your contract, this is
Two-week's notice. Your last performance
is February 6th.

I ran up the stairs to Louis's dressing room and pushed open the door. He was sitting in his shorts reading *Variety*. I couldn't speak so I just thrust the letter in front of him. He took it and his mouth fell open.

"I don't believe it," he said. "You've been doing so well."

He got me to sit down, and we went over the weeks since the opening in Hartford. We tried to find some incident that could have triggered the firing, but we couldn't. The performances had gone well, and I had gotten all my laughs. I never did get applause on my exit again, but the other actors told me the part never did. If anything, there seemed to be a shocked silence after my scene. I attributed it to the obnoxiousness of the character.

By the time we left Hartford, I had lost my voice completely. With all the aspirin I had been taking, I was barely aware of dragging my bags through the railway station. With the wartime jam and no red caps, I just barely managed to get on the train for New Haven where we had to change for Philadelphia. Louis suggested we still room together, so he'd gotten us into the Ritz- Carlton hotel. It sounded grand, but it was just a small hotel and only fifteen dollars a week.

I went to bed as soon as we got into the room and spent the next several weeks there, except for when I was doing the show or having a doctor paint my throat. The eight performances a week irritated it, so I never got my voice to sound quite right. The stage manager criticized something I had done wrong almost every time I came off stage, but he finally stopped doing it, so I felt more confident. But I never believed I'd really become the character.

After we had talked about all this, Louis said, "There must be some mistake. Go downstairs and speak to the stage manager. After all, he hired you."

I stood in front of the tall desk in the wings where the stage manager ran the show. The little man sat on a high stool, his face in darkness since the only light was a small clip-on that illuminated the script. He didn't even try to be kind.

"You had bad luck," he said. "Somebody from the New York office came to see the show and thought you were wrong for the part."

"But you knew that from the beginning," I said.

"Well, I thought you'd work into it, but you just didn't get any better."

I was relieved in a way. I hated the character I had to play. I'd had to grit my teeth each time I went onstage, take a deep breath and just scream my way through the scene. I knew the laughs I got were built in and anyone could have gotten them. As for the applause, it must have been the shock the audience had felt after watching a maniac run around the stage for several minutes. At least I'd only have to do sixteen more performances. But now I'd have to face the embarrassment of having the whole company know that I was fired. I also would have to figure out what I was going to do next, but I would not, under any circumstances, go back home.

The actors were wonderful. They all said it was terrible and totally unfair. They told me how good I had gotten in the part. They came up with elaborate excuses to help me gain my self-esteem. The leading lady suggested a perfect solution. She said that the management must have closed one of their other shows and suddenly had to find a job for one of the actors they had under contract. Everyone reminded me that I was now a member of Actor's Equity, so it would be much easier to get a job in another play.

I was sitting in my dressing room feeling almost triumphant from what everyone said. The boy who shared the room with me said, "You're a wonderful actor. They never should have fired you." I thanked him. "By the way," the boy said, "can I have your makeup kit since you won't be using it again?"

I rushed out and slammed the door. I stood against a yellowed wall of the hallway that was brashly lit by bare bulbs in metal cages. The tears I had held back all night poured down my face. So *that's what they all think, that I'm no good and I'll never act again. Well, they're wrong.* When I had cried myself out, I went back into the dressing room to get ready for the performance.

Chapter 36

After the show, Louis became the older brother I had always wanted my own brother to be. "You're going to New York to be an actor," he said. "That's what you told us you always wanted to be." He sat me down and outlined a plan. "I was going to go into New York several times after the performance anyway to see my parents and some friends," he said, "and now you'll come with me. We'll stay with my folks in Jersey City, so it won't cost you anything. Then in the daytime, we'll take the tube to New York and I'll show you how to look for work. You're still not draft age. There are so many jobs opening up as guys are taken into the service. It's a snap." Louis made it all seem so easy, but I kept thinking of my parents' reaction to me being fired. Maybe I could get a job before I had to tell them.

On Wednesday night after the show, Louis and I caught a train and went to Jersey City. His parents had a small, neat house outside the town. It was two in the morning, but they were waiting for us. They acted as if we were slightly late for a party. Louis's mother was a tiny bird-like woman with hair dyed jet black and a great resemblance to the woman she told me was her idol, Mrs. Arthur Murray. Louis's father was a big, quiet man who was in the construction business. His main interest in life seemed to be his wife who he looked at with adoration and amazement.

"Let's have a drink," Louis's mother said as soon as we were introduced. We all went down to the basement that was outfitted like a South Sea Island barroom. After several drinks, Pinky, as his mother insisted that I call her, danced and sang, "Arthur Murray Taught Me Dancing in a Hurry." She had a voice like a faulty radiator, but her dancing looked very professional. I somehow felt I'd stumbled onto the set of *You Can't Take It with You.*

Louis and I set out for New York the next day. He took me to Greenwich Village where he thought I might find an inexpensive room. First, we went to see two of his friends who lived opposite the New School of Social Research. Louis thought they might know of something for rent in the neighborhood. Marie and Madeline had just graduated Smith College and were rooming together. Marie was an actress, very pretty in an old-fashioned way, and Madeline was a writer, tall and plain-looking behind her large glasses.

They both fell on Louis, kissing him, running their hands through his thick hair, exclaiming how wonderful he looked and only stopped when he managed to introduce them to me. I felt rather shy, but they soon had me sitting on the sofa sipping a cup of tea beneath a huge print of people picnicking by a river. They all went into the bedroom to talk. Louis and I had never discussed our private lives, but I wondered if he was having a relationship with Marie. I looked around. I'd never seen so many books in French as well as English. The furniture was delicate, and everything looked antique.

When they came back, I was the center of attention. Louis had obviously told them about me being fired and they were determined to help. They said they'd seen a sign on Tenth Street for a room to rent and thought we should take a look at it.

"You'd be right near us," Marie said. "Everyone comes here for dinner and you just chip in. That way we could keep an eye on you and be sure you were eating enough."

When we left, Louis said he was glad Marie had taken me under her wing so quickly. He also told me that Madeline was born in New York and from a very good family. That was why there were so many antiques in the apartment.

We spotted the placard "For Rent" in a window with a dirty green shade and a house badly in need of paint. An old drudge took us up several flights of stairs in semi-darkness to a door in the back that she unlocked. She turned on a floor lamp beside a cot and then backed out so the two of us could get in. There were only a few feet between the bed and the dingy wall. We stood there almost touching each other in the tiny space. The acrid smell from the heat was nauseating, and I just wanted to get out into the air again.

"How much is it?" I heard Louis ask.

"Four dollars a week, two weeks in advance," the old woman muttered from the hall.

I pulled the shade up in the window thinking it might bring in some cheer, but it opened onto an air shaft. "I think you'd better take it," Louis said. "You'll be near Marie and Madeline. You can always get something else later."

I counted out eight dollars in the woman's arthritic hand and told her I'd be there on Sunday February 7th. She didn't even look at me. I had the impression that no one stayed there very long if they could help it.

The next trip into New York, Louis took me to Times Square and showed me a newsstand where I could buy a copy of *Show Business*. It came out once a week and listed all the available acting jobs. The wind was so strong that we couldn't keep the paper open to read it, so we went into a Nedicks on Forty-Second Street for a cup of coffee. With a pencil, Louis helped me mark all of the places I planned to go, then I bracketed them according to location. There was enough time to go to several places before we had to take the train back to Philadelphia. At least I got a taste of "Making the rounds" as Louis told me it was called. The two agents' offices we visited were crowded with actors. When we stood near a desk where a girl sat typing, she looked up at us and said in a monotone, "Nothing today." I thought it seemed so easy. It was all just a matter of time before I got a job.

I realized I would have to tell my parents about leaving the play, so I wrote a long letter putting the best face on it that I could. I described the furnished room as if it were in a fancy magazine. I told them about being promised a reading as a replacement in *Life with Father*. (That actually happened on a later foray into New York.) I reminded them of how much I wanted to be an actor. "I know I will be a success," I wrote.

For the first time, they seemed to understand completely. They must have realized that I badly needed their support and confidence if I was going to recover from the shock of being fired. They wrote back that they agreed with me going to New York and giving acting a try. They enclosed a clipping from my high school newspaper entitled "Mr. Cinderella." It said that I was on my way to stardom. If I'd ever thought for a moment of going back home, I sure couldn't do it now.

The night of my final performance, Louis and two of the girls from the show took me to Stouffer's for dinner. I had a fruit cup, steak, vegetables, and Dutch apple pie with ice cream, all for a dollar. They even insisted on paying. I felt like I was having my last meal before being electrocuted, so I ate every bite.

My scene went better than it ever had. The stage manager called out to me as I headed to my dressing room. I went over to his desk. He looked at me for a moment, and then said grudgingly, "If you'd done it that way when the office was here, they wouldn't have fired you."

I thanked him and walked away. The rest of the evening was spent trying to make everyone feel good as they came to me with long faces and condolences. After the show, since the play was going to move to Washington the next morning, the actors had to put their makeup kits in a huge communal trunk. I carried mine under my arm as I walked to the stage door on my way out. Two of the boys were placing their kits in the bottom of the trunk. They looked up, embarrassed to see me still holding mine, then quickly looked away. I went out the door with my head held high.

When I got back to our room at the hotel, Louis was waiting for me. He was smoking a cigarette, which he seldom did, and he seemed very uneasy. I figured he didn't know quite what to say about me finally leaving the play. "Don't worry," I said. "I'll be fine. I've got the girls as friends, so I won't be alone, and I know I'll get work."

"That's not what's on my mind," he said.

"Well, then what is wrong? Did I do something?"

"I love you," Louis blurted out. "I could never say it before because you were ill and going through so much with the play. I didn't want to make you get even more upset. But I couldn't let you go without telling you. I don't expect you to feel the same way."

I was stunned. I'd never really thought of Louis that way, but of course I'd had too much on my mind. I just looked at him, not knowing what to say. He'd been such a great friend that I didn't want to hurt him. Roger kept going through my mind. I'd thought, as month after month had passed with no word from him, that he must have wanted to end our relationship. But why hadn't he written and told me so? On the other hand, what if something had happened to him? I wasn't free to think about anyone else. I couldn't go into it all with Louis.

"Louis, I think you're wonderful, but I just feel dead inside. It isn't that I don't have feelings for you, I just don't have them for anyone right now."

"That's all right. I just wanted to tell you how I felt before we separated, and to ask you to think about it while you're in New York and I'm still on tour. I'm just hoping that when the play closes and I come back, we can live together and that someday, you'll love me."

I walked over to Louis and put my arms around him. "We're going to be apart for a long time. You know how much I think of you. Let's write each other and get to know each other better. And who knows what can happen?"

Chapter 37

Lying on my back with my eyes closed, I kept hoping I'd fall asleep again. I clutched the stiff top sheet with my hands and tried to think of something that would calm me down, but as much as I tried to push it out of my head, it was still there. This was my first day in New York and I was alone with hardly any money. I looked at my watch. It was only six o'clock and I'd had very little sleep. The bed was too small for me and it felt like I was stretched out on a board. The smell of the oil heat had closed up my sinuses, but as much as it gave evidence that the furnace was working, the room was ice cold.

I decided I might as well get ready for the day. I walked down the hall to the communal bathroom. I was afraid I would wake everyone in the rooming house if I took a shower, so I ran water into the tub. The bottom was so stained that it did no good no matter how hard I rubbed with my washcloth. I sank into the lukewarm water and faced a window that was painted black. I realized that since I couldn't see out, and the window in my room faced an air shaft, I would never know what the weather was like until I got outdoors. I had to find another place to live.

When I walked out the door and down the steps of the stoop, a rush of wind blew open my coat and made me shiver. I quickly buttoned it and thought, *I hope I can get through the winter with this.* It was a herringbone tweed that was meant for the fall, not February, and the cold seemed to go right through it. But it was my only good coat, so I'd had my mother send it to me. Louis had told me to always dress up to see the agents. I had on my best dark suit and black shoes, with the soles worn thin. There were remnants of dirty snow in the gutters, but nothing on the sidewalks, so I figured I could get away without wearing rubbers. I thought they would make me look shoddy.

I tried to get my bearings at the corner of Tenth Street and Sixth Avenue. In the distance was the Empire State Building, and I knew that was Thirty-Fourth Street, so if I walked in that direction, I would come to Fourteenth Street where there was a subway entrance. The only two places I remembered from my subway rides with Louis were Fourteenth Street and Times Square at Forty-Second Street. In order to go uptown, I would get off at Forty-Second Street and walk. If I were going to Fifty-Seventh Street, I had to walk fifteen blocks. Later, I learned the subway system that made my life easier.

I went to a newsstand at Times Square and bought *Show Business*. It was only eight o'clock and the offices weren't open, so I went to a Nedicks and had breakfast. For ten cents I got an orange drink, one whole wheat doughnut and a cup of coffee. I sat underlining job notices until the counterman told me I'd have to order something else if I planned to stay there. I couldn't afford it, so I walked around Times Square until ten. The place had none of the glamour I saw in the movies. It was dirty, crowded and sleazy. All the people raced to get somewhere. I seemed the only one with no destination. I stood in front of the Times building. It seemed like the four winds, from each point of the compass, met there. A man in a heavy pea jacket and earmuffs was putting out papers in a newsstand. I noticed they were from all over the world and I went to the racks to see if *The Boston Globe* was there. It was, and I felt a sharp pang of homesickness. I put it out of my head and walked in the building to get warm.

At three in the afternoon, I stood in a line at the stage door of the Playhouse Theater. It wasn't quite as cold in the alley between the buildings. I was happy just to be in a place where there might be work. All day I had gone from office to office where secretaries behind glass windows said, "Nothing today." Sometimes there were crudely lettered signs with the same words. But I'd read in *Show Business* that actors were wanted for the play *Janie* at the Playhouse, so I waited. I got in the door after an hour, when I was quite numb. I was ready with my story that I had left *Junior Miss* because I didn't want to tour when a man came up to me and looked me up and down.

He turned to a younger man, who was holding a clipboard, and said, "Okay." I was asked for my name and phone number. I couldn't believe my luck. It looked like they were going to give me a reading for the play.

"Be here at eight tonight," the younger man said and turned away. I wanted to ask him if I'd get a chance to look over a script before I read, but I was afraid of looking like I didn't know my way around. I went back to the Village and sat in my claustrophobic room until it was time to go uptown again.

I was fifteen minutes early and the old stage doorman greeted me with a surly voice. "What do you want?"

"I was told to be here at eight," I said. "I'm a little early."

"You can go down to the basement," he said and pointed, "through that door."

Beneath the stage was a cavernous room lined with benches and metal lockers. I sat down and waited. Before long, other young men began to arrive. They all seemed to know each other, and they joked and talked. Some of them played cards but none of them paid any attention to me.

When the older man, who I figured was the stage manager, walked in holding the clipboard, he made a beeline for me. "I hear you were early," he said. "I thought I told you eight o'clock."

"I had to be in the neighborhood," I said afraid of seeming too eager.

"Come with me," the man said. We walked over to a long clothes rack jammed with Army clothes. He went through them, peering at the name tags in the subdued light, until he pulled one uniform out. "Here," he handed it to me, "try this on." I looked for a place to go but the man said, "Nobody's going to look at you. You can change right here." I was afraid to ask any questions, so I took off my clothes and folded them on a bench. The uniform fit perfectly. "It looks good," the stage manager said. "We figured you were the same size as the guy who left. Now, don't leave any money in your clothes and be here every night at nine. Some of the guys come in earlier, if they have nothing to do, but you don't have to. You go onstage at nine-twenty and you get a dollar a night right after you come off."

"What do I do?" I asked.

"You've seen the play, haven't you?" the man asked.

I was afraid if I said I hadn't, they'd pick someone else. "Oh sure," I said.

"Good," said the man, "so just follow the others and make a lot of noise." He took a tag that had been on the costume and wrote my name on it. "Put this in your pocket," he said and disappeared up the stairs.

I sat in my uniform and waited. I had hung up my clothes and taken the money out of them as I'd been instructed. I didn't want to admit to any of the others that I didn't know what I was doing, so I just sat quietly. More and more young men arrived, undressed and put on uniforms from the rack. They unpinned the name tags and put them in their pockets, as I had. I couldn't believe my good fortune. One day in New York and I was going to be on the Broadway stage. *But what am I going to do?*

Finally, the stage manager's assistant came down the stairs. "Let's go, guys," he said, and everyone started to follow him. I went with them and thought desperately *What do I say? What do I do? I know I'm going to make a terrible fool of myself.*

The group assembled at a door in the back of the scenery. I opened my mouth to ask the boy next to me what to do, but the stage manager pointed his finger, and everyone started to yell and laugh. The door to the stage opened and I was swept along with all the others. For a moment, the spotlights blinded me. Then I looked right at the audience. I realized that the curtain was coming down as we all walked onstage. We were only there for a minute. Then I heard loud applause.

Afterward, I lined up with the other actors to get my dollar. As he handed me the money, the stage manager said, "Make some more noise tomorrow. Act like you're going to a party."

I had to smile to myself. I had just made my Broadway debut.

Chapter 38

I was trying to get through my second night in the dingy furnished room. It wasn't really even furnished. There was no room for a bureau, so I had to store my two suitcases under the bed and pull them out whenever I needed anything. Even though the window was sealed shut, I felt the draft on my head as I lay in bed. All my father's admonitions came back as I lay awake. *What if I got sick? I'd have to go home.*

Louis had called me earlier in the evening from Washington. He had written down the telephone number of the pay phone on the first floor. The landlady yelled my name and I thought she was going to complain about something. Instead, it was Louis wanting to surprise me and wish me well. He said he missed me, and then told me my name was listed in big letters with the other actors on the front of the theater. Obviously, they hadn't gotten word that I'd been replaced. "So, in a way, you're still appearing in Washington," he said. I had to laugh. We talked for a few minutes and I told him about *Janie* and said everything was going well.

But after another night of not being able to sleep with the noise of the furnace going on and off, I had to find something else. With the eight dollars a week from the play and some war bonds I had sent to my parents from my salary, maybe I could afford a little more than four dollars a week.

I had seen a notice of a rental in *Show Business* the day before, but it was for forty dollars a month. After the hideous night, I thought I'd at least take a look. I phoned and made an appointment. In the middle of the block, I saw the awning with the number "Forty" printed on it in white against the dark green. I stopped for a moment to get up my courage, took a deep breath, and said to myself, *you just have to act like you belong and no one will question you.* I pushed back my shoulders and walked briskly to the door.

"Good morning," said the doorman.

"I'm here to see Mr. Broner," I replied.

"That's the penthouse," the old man said, "go right in." He held open the door and I walked through. An elevator man stood waiting. "This gentleman is for Mr. Broner, Fred," the doorman said as I got into the elevator.

I kept thinking there must be a mistake, but I had asked over the phone if the rent was forty dollars and the man had said yes. Maybe I'd gotten confused since the address was also forty. How could it be so cheap with a doorman and an elevator man on Fifty-Fifth Street right off Fifth Avenue? The gate opened and I stepped out into a narrow hall with a door at the end. "That one there," the elevator man pointed, and I rang the bell.

A huge man shaped like a hippopotamus greeted me. "You must be Mr. Shayne," he said. "Come in." I walked into a vault-like room with an enormous studio window looking out at the New York skyline. There was a grand piano covered with sheets of music that were also scattered all over the floor. I couldn't believe my good fortune and thought immediately how I could clean it up and make it wonderful. "Needless to say," the large man said, "this is not the place I'm renting. It's right next door."

I followed him, watching his great hips waddle and suddenly noticed that he was in his stocking feet. "This is it," Mr. Broner said. I saw a large room painted white, with a black cement floor, and two windows with wire mesh that looked out at a narrow balcony and the side of a building. "That's the Rockefeller Apartments. Gertrude Lawrence lives in that one with the terrace."

I couldn't believe it. I had stood in the freezing cold in Boston for an hour waiting to get her autograph. Now, I could reach out and almost touch her if she walked outside. I examined the room carefully. There was a studio couch with a royal blue fitted cover and a white dresser. "Is this all?" I asked.

"I haven't shown you the kitchen and the bathroom yet," he said as if he'd forgotten all about them. He took me out to the hall again where there were several other doors I hadn't noticed. One opened up to a small toilet, another to a shower, and the third to a small refrigerator with a two-burner stove and a sink. I realized I'd have to wash in the kitchen and walk out into the hall in my pajamas. "Nobody else would use these but you," he said. I thought that was at least better than the bathroom I shared with six people now. "I'm a musician, and I practice all day, so I have to rent this room as well, because of all the noise I make. That's why I'm charging so little."

I thought, *it's hardly the penthouse of my dreams, but anything to get away from the filth of the place I'm in.* "How about thirty-five dollars a month?" I heard myself say. "There isn't any furniture."

"I can get you a few more things," he said. "Okay, I don't want to waste any more time away from my music seeing people. You can have it."

That night I went to dinner at Marie and Madeline's. There were several older men and women who talked about Kafka and Eliot, writers I knew nothing about, so I didn't say a word. Finally, sensing how uncomfortable I was, Marie asked me what I had done that day. I told them of my adventure—seeing the ad, not believing the building and the doorman, and then finding the misshapen musician padding around in his stocking feet. Everybody laughed and made me feel welcome. Madeline immediately said, "I have so much stuff in storage in the cellar. There are old draperies and some chairs. Let's go down right after dinner."

I had to get to the theater by nine to walk-on in *Janie* so we barely had time to look at the furniture, but I chose some blue striped draperies that matched the color of the studio couch, a gate-legged dining table, a chair Madeline said had belonged to Napoleon's son, two French maps, and dishes that didn't match. Marie said she would arrange to load them in her car the next day if it was all right with Broner. I paid her my share of dinner and they both kissed me on the cheek as we said goodbye.

I called my parents after the show and told them the good news. They seemed pleased and said they'd send me twenty dollars instead of cashing two war bonds. Mother also said she'd send several heavy sweaters that I could wear under my thin overcoat.

I was settled in my new apartment within the week. There was more heat in the room, so I was no longer cold at night. I was closer to the theatrical offices, so I could move about more easily and get out earlier to make the rounds. I saved the money for the subway, but since rent was so expensive, I had to cut down on my eating. I continued to have the ten-cent breakfast at Nedicks and a hot-dog-and-bean dish for dinner at the Automat that was only twenty cents. I also started working at the Stage Door Canteen to help with the war effort. I didn't get paid, but I got to eat some of the leftover food.

The package arrived from my mother. Inside, wrapped in my sweaters, was the cut glass decanter I had managed to wheedle out of my grandmother. There was a note from my mother saying she knew I planned to have it in my penthouse in New York and she wished me well. I put some Welch's grape juice in the decanter (since it was cheaper than wine) and set it on the dining room table.

I had left Louis a message with my new number and the news of the apartment. So, on the last day *Junior Miss* would play in Washington before they continued their tour, Broner gave me a note saying that Louis had called and wanted me to telephone him after the matinee. There was an extension phone in my room that I was allowed to use if I kept track of the money for any calls. Broner also offered to take messages, knowing that I was looking for work in the theater.

When I called Louis, he said again how much he missed me, and that Marie and Madeline thought I was charming and funny. I talked of agents I'd seen and my hope of a few promised readings. Actually, things were looking bleaker than when I'd arrived, but there was no reason to burden Louis.

"Listen," he said, "I have something funny to tell you. The strangest thing happened last night. You remember I told you your name was in big letters on the poster outside the theater?"

"Yes," I said. "There was a mistake and they hadn't listed my replacement instead. Why? Is the guy making trouble about it?"

"No, nothing like that. Two Army officers came backstage, before the show last night, asking to see you. The stage doorman told them you weren't in the company. They were drunk and one of them evidently kept saying to the other, 'You've got to see this kid. He's so talented and he can sing too.' He wouldn't believe you'd left the show, so one of the actors who overheard came and got me, knowing that I was still in touch with you. I went down and told this guy that you were now in New York, and if he wanted to reach you, I'd give him your address and the phone number." Louis paused for a moment, but I didn't say anything. He went on, "The officer got very annoyed and they both left. Have you any idea who they were?"

"No," I replied. "They were probably friends of my brother's. Did the officer take my address?"

"No," Louis answered. "He said he didn't want it."

We went back to talking about any shows casting in New York. Actors always gossip and Louis had hoped to hear something that might help me get a reading. There wasn't anything promising. I thanked him again for introducing me to Marie and Madeline, and for all his help. We promised to write and speak to each other often.

I hung up the phone and sat down in Napoleon's son's chair. *So, Roger was alive.* What a relief. So often I had prayed that he was safe and just didn't want to contact me. And here, at last, was the answer. But why? In all these months, why couldn't he have written and told me it was over? Did he think I wouldn't be capable of dealing with it? Louis said he called me a kid. Of course, he had last seen me when I had just turned sixteen. Now I was headed to eighteen and on my own in New York. I had changed so much. I felt sad realizing I no longer had any feelings for him. He'd managed to kill them by avoiding me for so long. Why did he even bother to go backstage if he didn't want to see me? Probably he wanted to show off that he knew an actor in a Broadway play. Did he want me to sing "Jenny" again? I didn't feel angry. If anything, I would always be grateful to

Roger for opening me up to a life I wouldn't have known without him. But now, I didn't need his help or his guidance anymore, or his love. I didn't blame him. It was a good feeling to pull the curtain down on something that was no longer a part of my life.

I looked around my little room. It wasn't much, but it was mine. And it was the present, not the past. So much had happened since I'd set out for Falmouth almost two years ago. There were many good things and some bad as well. Suddenly an image came into my head: Marla Forbes, standing in the pouring rain saying goodbye to me at that first meeting I had with her at the summer stock theater in Rockport. I remember she reached through the open car window and took hold of my arm.

Like an oracle at Delphi she announced, "The rain may pass."

Epilogue

I did get to Broadway in a leading role opposite Martita Hunt in *The Madwoman of Chaillot*, but as predicted by the actress in Boston, it took me five years. In that time, I waited tables, ushered in theaters, was a secretary for a doctor, returned to radio announcing at WNYC in New York, toured the United States in Shakespearean plays with Maurice Evans and Katharine Cornell and, when I was rejected from the Army because of an ear problem, I went to the Pacific for the USO with *Junior Miss*, in the very same role that I had been fired from.

I was a leading man in early television. I even sang and danced opposite Lena Horne in *Jamaica* on Broadway. I left acting to produce television specials like *The House Without a Christmas Tree* and *The Bourne Identity*. I was an early casting director with movies like *All the President's Men* and *Catch-22*. I became President of Warner Brothers Television for ten years and left to read the books I'd never had time for... and to write.

I spent years in analysis trying to change, after a marriage and a five-year affair with the actress Mary Fickett. I finally decided that just being myself brought true happiness.

Now I live in a house with a beautiful garden like the one I had always imagined when I was a child. I share it with the artist Norman Sunshine who for so many years has been the answer to all my dreams.

I did buy my mother the mink stole she had always wanted, and I never heard from Roger again.

CPSIA information can be obtained
at www.ICGtesting.com
Printed in the USA
LVHW111446200920
666584LV00005B/100/J